How to Use Work Group Supervision to Improve Early Years Practice

How to Use Work Group Supervision to Improve Early Years Practice presents a new model for supervision as a collaborative process, and explores how this process can benefit practitioners at all stages in their career to reflect on and improve their own practice. Supported by detailed case studies which contextualise Work Group Supervision, Louis offers practical support which will help practitioners develop their knowledge and skills, and to work together to develop a shared understanding and more successful practice.

Louis covers a range of insightful topics to help practitioners utilise the Work Group Supervision method to improve their practice, including:

- What Work Group Supervision is and how it can help practitioners
- How to develop self-understanding and professional practice
- Theories on child observation, and using observation to tune into children
- The importance of respectful interactions as a leader and among peers

How to Use Work Group Supervision to Improve Early Years Practice is ideal for Early Years practitioners and teachers, managers of Early Years settings and students on courses for leadership in Early Childhood settings.

Stella Louis is an Early Years consultant and author based in the UK.

How to Use Work Group Supervision to Improve Early Years Practice

Stella Louis

LONDON AND NEW YORK

First edition published 2021
by Routledge
2 Park Square, Milton Park, Abingdon, Oxon, OX14 4RN

and by Routledge
52 Vanderbilt Avenue, New York, NY 10017

Routledge is an imprint of the Taylor & Francis Group, an informa business

© 2021 Stella Louis

The right of Stella Louis to be identified as author of this work has been asserted by her in accordance with sections 77 and 78 of the Copyright, Designs and Patents Act 1988.

All rights reserved. No part of this book may be reprinted or reproduced or utilised in any form or by any electronic, mechanical, or other means, now known or hereafter invented, including photocopying and recording, or in any information storage or retrieval system, without permission in writing from the publishers.

Trademark notice: Product or corporate names may be trademarks or registered trademarks, and are used only for identification and explanation without intent to infringe.

British Library Cataloguing-in-Publication Data
A catalogue record for this book is available from the British Library

Library of Congress Cataloging-in-Publication Data
A catalog record has been requested for this book

ISBN: 978-0-367-18460-5 (hbk)
ISBN: 978-0-367-18461-2 (pbk)
ISBN: 978-0-429-19644-7 (ebk)

Typeset in Optima
by Swales & Willis, Exeter, Devon, UK

For my darling daughter Hannah Louise, with love
July 2019

Contents

	About this book	xii
	Introduction	1
1	**Theorists of child observations**	4
	Friedrich Froebel's (1782–1852) contribution to Early Childhood education	4
	Susan Isaacs' contribution to Early Childhood education	7
	The Malting House School	8
	Jean Piaget's contributions to Early Childhood education	10
	Lev Vygotsky's contribution to Early Childhood education	12
	Language and thought	13
	Comparisons and contrasts about how children learn	15
	Sigmund Freud	16
	Anna Freud	17
	Psychoanalytic concepts	18
	Conclusion	19
	Bibliography	20
2	**The role of the Early Years educator and observation**	23
	Introduction	23
	Introducing the role of the Early Years educator	24
	The Early Years curriculum	26
	Observation practice in Early Years settings	28

	Child development: Learning in infants and young children	29
	Conclusion	32
	Bibliography	32
3	**What do we see when children play?**	**35**
	Unpicking play	36
	Storying	39
	Competence	39
	Block play: This is free-standing wooden block play	41
	Observing block play learning	42
	Conclusion	43
	Bibliography	44
4	**Schemas: The key to patterns of behaviour**	**45**
	What is a schema?	46
	Observing schemas	46
	Adults helping children to learn	47
	Identifying schemas	49
	The Trajectory schema	50
	The Rotation schema	51
	The Enclosing schema	51
	The Containing schema	52
	The Enveloping schema	52
	The Transporting schema	54
	The Positioning schema	54
	The Orientation schema	55
	Connecting and disconnecting schema	55
	Schema clusters	56
	The core and radial schema	56
	Evaluation and reflection	58
	Conclusion	59
	Bibliography	59
5	**What is supervision?**	**61**
	What is Work Group Supervision?	62
	Why supervision matters	63
	Conclusion	64
	Bibliography	64
6	**Implementing Work Group Supervision and bringing observational practice into focus using Work Group Supervision**	**66**
	How Early Years educators feel is important	66

	Supporting Early Years educators	67
	How leaders and managers show support is important	68
	Work Group Supervision	69
	Principles of Work Group Supervision	70
	Getting started	70
	Choosing a facilitator	71
	Record-keeping	72
	Frequency of Work Group Supervision	72
	Burnout	72
	Continuing Professional Development for Early Years educators	73
	Bringing observational practice into focus using Work Group Supervision	73
	Supervision	74
	Observation	74
	Work Group Supervision	75
	The facilitator	78
	Empowerment	80
	What are the challenges?	80
	What are the benefits?	81
	Conclusion	82
	Bibliography	83
7	**Group consultation**	**85**
	Vygotsky's social constructivist perspective	87
	Implications of Vygotsky's constructivist theory on group consultation processes	88
	Problem-solving approaches to group consultation	89
	Benefits and weaknesses of group consultation	91
	Psychoanalytic approaches	92
	Benefits and weaknesses of psychoanalytic approach	93
	Process Consultation	94
	Benefits and weaknesses of Process Consultation	95
	Conclusion	95
	Bibliography	96
8	**Work Group Supervision in practice: Developing pedagogy, self-understanding and teamwork**	**100**
	Stage 1: Part 1	102
	Stage 1: Part 2	104
	Stage 2	105
	Stage 3	105
	Stage 4	106

Developing pedagogy and self-understanding	108
Denise: Relationships with a key person	108
Kate: Knowing and communicating	109
Erica: Observing and responding	111
Julie: Learning together	112
Learning together as a team	114
Conclusion	117
Bibliography	117

9 Using observation to tune into children – and its challenges — 120

Why observe?	121
What to observe?	122
Supporting development and learning	123
Making learning visible	124
How to write observations?	125
Recognising significant development and learning	127
Reflective questions	128
Linking theory to practice	128
Conclusion	130
Bibliography	130

10 Respectful interactions are everything — 132

Getting to know children and building relationships with them	133
Respecting and appreciating children	133
Reflecting on the quality of interactions	134
Knowing when to intervene	135
What kind of support is appropriate?	136
Using observations to connect with children	137
Knowing when to interact and help	138
Effective interaction	138
Adult interaction and pedagogy	140
Involving children in their learning	141
Tuning into children	142
Involvement scales, well-being scales and observing deep-level learning	143
Conclusion	146
Bibliography	146

11 Developing professional practice through Work Group Supervision — 149

Understanding child development is key	150
Misunderstandings about implementing the curriculum	151

Providing pedagogical support	152
Refreshing and updating knowledge	152
Conclusion	153
Bibliography	154
Index	156

About this book

Because of the nature of the job, Early Years educators may find they have a problem if they do not understand children's behaviour. In this context, Work Group Supervision is a powerful tool for supporting day-to-day practice, performance and understanding. Early Years educators can often work in isolation without supervision. They tend to feel responsible for their observations and children making progress, but they may have little or no knowledge of child development and the importance of play. Sometimes this need is not met, depending on the organisation that they work for.

This book is made up of three interconnecting sections. The first section outlines the vital knowledge and understanding of child development required and the role of the Early Years educator in observation and understanding the structure of play. The second section explores the purposes and different models of group consultation and a new model of Work Group Supervision designed for Early Years settings to support and contain the emotional aspect of educators' work. The third and final part reviews the impact of Work Group Supervision on many aspects of professional practice, including educators' emotional engagement with children.

This book will help educators to articulate and recognise developing learning, locate themselves in their practice, and understand what they bring to the observing process. Some educators may lack confidence in their professional knowledge and will need support in developing their observation skills and an understanding of how children learn and develop. This book will also look at key aspects vital for developing observational practice, bringing together theory and practice from the practitioners' perspective using case study examples.

This book is aimed at Early Years sector head teachers and senior leaders, teachers, managers and practitioners in maintained nursery schools and private, voluntary or independent settings, who want to ensure that support is provided to broaden educators' knowledge of child development and how children learn.

About this book

Chapter 1 explores the history of Early Childhood development, highlighting the work of Friedrich Froebel, Susan Isaacs, Lev Vygotsky, Jean Piaget and many more important theorists who still influence how we teach infants and young children today. It also discusses how their theories still show us possibilities within the detail of what might be noticed in our observations, as well as the absence of behaviours that are thought of as significant.

Chapter 2 examines the highly skilled and complex role of the Early Years educator and the task of observation, and highlights how vital it is for educators to have knowledge of child development and curriculum, as it relates to the requirement to support learning. It also discusses how educators can use what they have learned from observing children to support them. In this chapter you will find universal principles that represent the knowledge, skills and understanding required to make effective observations of infants and young children.

Chapter 3 looks more closely at the complexities and connections involved in children's play and discusses the importance of managers and educators understanding how play is structured, so as to implement Work Group Supervision effectively. This chapter challenges managers to lead by example and has been designed to help them to assess their own knowledge.

Chapter 4 considers schemas as a biological learning mechanism and looks at how recognising and understanding these schematic patterns across a range of experiences can support educators to provide more effective learning experiences for children.

Chapter 5 moves away from child development and the structure of play and discusses the role of supervision in providing pedagogical support to Early Years educators. This chapter includes a discussion about why supervision matters and how Work Group Supervision can be used in an Early Years setting to enable educators to reflect on their work and also combine the group supervision with observations. A new model of Work Group Supervision is introduced where managers will discover how to encourage the group members to collaborate and learn from each other through problem solving and action planning.

Chapter 6 looks extensively at different models of group consultation and how they can help to reduce burnout among educators while improving their professional practice. It explores how group consultation can empower educators to discuss and share their concerns about observations with colleagues, receive feedback – for example, about how to handle challenging or difficult behaviour – and provide opportunities to share knowledge and practice.

Chapter 7 draws on case study examples which illustrate the impact of attending Work Group Supervision. These demonstrate the participants' desire and motivation to challenge themselves as they begin to gain confidence and enjoyment from attending Work Group Supervision. This chapter takes the reader through each stage of the process, revealing growth and advancement in knowledge and self-understanding.

About this book

Chapter 8 examines some of the hidden challenges involved with observing infants and young children – knowing what significant learning looks like and how to record it, and the ability to apply theoretical knowledge to everyday practice. This chapter includes criteria for writing observations. It also looks at the role of Work Group Supervision in supporting Early Years educators to develop specific aspects of their observational practice.

Chapter 9 considers some of the challenges concerning Early Years educators' relationships and interactions with children and makes the important link between how the educator relates to the children and how this shapes their observations of them. It illustrates how observing children can help educators to build these relationships, drawing on case study examples, and considers different ways of interacting with children that enable them to be successful learners.

Chapter 10 addresses some important challenges faced by Early Years educators in understanding the observation process and mediating what they bring to it. It also explores how Work Group Supervision can provide professional training and support.

This book has been written to help Early Years educators who work with infants and young children to understand how children learn as well as how to embed the principles of Work Group Supervision into their practice. Educators' observations are important. The more educators observe, the better they get to know and understand children and how best to support them. The challenge is to take full advantage of the professional development opportunities that Work Group Supervision offers, particularly the divulge of useful information about children's learning, gained through careful observation.

Introduction

This book has been written in response to the accountability pressures endemic within the Early Years field. These can lead to a tendency for some educators to interpret the curriculum and their matching learning goals in narrow and restrictive ways, with only a shallow predetermined understanding of children's development and learning. This puts good practice in jeopardy, fragmenting and misrepresenting the complex and interconnected ways in which children learn. As a result, it can switch attention away from examining what children are actually doing and can reduce observations to a "tick list" in a technical operation. In so doing, these "tick lists" of curriculums and learning goals satisfy the perceived accountability and data requirements, rather than meeting the needs or the best interests of the children.

Many leaders or managers may already supervise staff on issues relating to performance, responsibility and accountability. So, why provide Work Group Supervision? Work Group Supervision gives educators coaching, support and training in a series of monthly facilitated group discussions, in which the whole team is encouraged to come together to take a holistic view of young children's active development and learning, underpinned by child development theories. During Work Group Supervision, educators present what is known and understood about the children attending the setting. In these discussions, educators are guided to examine the significance of children's play and explorations and the diverse and interconnected ways in which they learn. The facilitator listens attentively in order to identify what is not known and what the educator is having difficulties with. These can then be supported with guidance and encouragement from others. Work Group Supervision can play an important part in every educator's practice, because it provides pedagogical support by allowing for regular time to think about and locate each child's experiences within a wider network of relationships, quality of interactions and environment.

Introduction

It is vital that all those working with infants and young children have a sound knowledge of child development. Educators must understand the different biological stages of development that children go through and they need to know that each stage depends on what learning has gone before. It is important that educators understand that each stage needs to be culturally experienced by children fully, without being rushed. Educators must also have an understanding of the curriculum and the structure of play, particularly if they are going to use play for assessment purposes, to know what is expected and how they can support development and learning. They must also understand the ways in which children symbolise or express ideas and achieve their own goals.

An educator's role is highly skilled and complex, requiring knowledge of child development and how play is structured, together with an ability to observe, support and extend learning as it develops. This is vital if educators are to gain a picture of each child's capacity and interests. If Work Group Supervision is to be implemented effectively, an in-depth understanding of child development theories and knowledge of the structure of play is required.

Observations are a key part of the educator's role – we all see and value different things when observing children and the lenses through which educators view their observational work reflect what they focus on and value and what they ignore. This is where Work Group Supervision comes into play, supporting educators to question and think more deeply about what they see and hear children doing. Work Group Supervision provides the means of supporting and empowering educators to make informed judgements about a child's development without being overburdened by paperwork. That is why the first part of this book begins with chapters on child development theories, the role of the Early Years educator and observation, and examines what we see when children play. Schemas, the key to patterns of behaviour, are also explored throughout the book. It is important to start with this essential knowledge and understanding as this will enable leaders and managers to implement Work Group Supervision more effectively.

Support, coaching and training should be offered to educators through Work Group Supervision to ensure that they understand how to effectively implement and make better sense of the curriculum and what to expect from children. Educators need opportunities to reflect on their practice and update their knowledge and this book is intended to help leaders and managers provide practical pedagogical support for educators to develop observational skills and techniques – and much more. The way in which Work Group Supervision is facilitated really matters – it determines the degree of support that takes place and therefore the extent to which scaffolding of an individual's learning can guide the group's learning and the development of confident and knowledgeable educators.

There is an obvious symmetry between what is expected of educators in relation to the children – for example, to be thoughtful about their ideas – and what is expected of the facilitator in relation to the educators, to also be thoughtful about their ideas, concerns and anxieties. The book includes chapters on why Work Group Supervision matters and a key chapter on the purpose, models and different forms of this group consultation approach.

Using case study examples, this book will explore the effect on observational practice of attending Work Group Supervision as it relates to the inside knowledge of being an educator, as well as reviewing the impact on the educator's ability to notice, recognise, respond and reflect on the process of observing young children. Professional dialogue with colleagues is a powerful contributor to learning, not least because it can increase confidence and knowledge while also providing opportunities for those attending to think about what they bring to observing.

Theorists of child observations

How do we know how children develop and learn? Why are children so challenging at 2 years old? Why do children need to repeat things? These questions have all been studied by Johann Pestalozzi, Friedrich Froebel, Margaret McMillan, John Dewey, Rudolf Steiner, Maria Montessori, Susan Isaacs, Jean Piaget, Lev Vygotsky, John Bowlby, Loris Malaguzzi and Chris Athey. They have given us useful theories about how children develop and learn and have also contributed to our understanding of the subject. These theorists provide educators with a useful framework for encouraging them to reflect upon their own practice – and their ideas are still very relevant today.

Friedrich Froebel's (1782–1852) contribution to Early Childhood education

Born on 21 April 1782, Friedrich Froebel was a German educator. He studied as an apprentice fosterer where he developed his ideas about nature and children and the importance of engaging in it. In 1799, he first studied mathematics and began teaching at the Anton Gruner school in 1805. Two years later, aged 25, he outlined his desire to open his own school. From 1808–1810, Froebel studied and worked under Johann Pestalozzi in Switzerland.

Pestalozzi believed that education was the key to creating a just society. He developed a whole child approach that focused on "heads, hands and hearts". However, Froebel believed that spirituality was missing from Pestalozzi's theory. He eventually abandoned some aspects of Pestalozzi's approach due to a disagreement over the compartmentalisation of subjects, believing instead that all learning was integrated, as each area of learning affects and influences others. Unlike Pestalozzi, Froebel advocated that learning starts at birth. Froebel was interested in the wholeness and unity in all things and in 1814 spent two years studying crystallography and mineralogy. By 1816, Froebel had founded the Universal German Educational Institute and formed a school in Keilhau. At this school, Froebel introduced worthwhile educational toys which he named gifts and occupations. Drawing on his knowledge of mathematics and crystallography, Froebel developed a set of wooden "gifts", which he numbered 1–6. Carefully thinking about children's development and learning, the gifts have a developmental sequence. On their progression and order he says: "I have already intimated that each following play thing is necessarily presupposed in and required by the preceding" (Froebel, 1899:319).

Froebel's educational toys are:

- Gift 1: Set of multi-coloured yarn balls with strings (for the infant)
- Gift 2: Wooden ball, cylinder and cube (for the 1–2-year-old)
- Gift 3: Set of eight small wooden cubes (blocks) (for the 2–3-year-old)
- Gift 4: Set of eight small wooden planks (blocks) (for the 2–3-year-old)
- Gift 5: Set of wooden blocks that includes cubes, planks and triangles (for the 3–4-year-old)
- Gift 6: Set of more complex wooden blocks that also includes cubes, planks and triangles (for the 4–5-year-old) (Quinn, 2013)

What Froebel calls "occupations" are activities such as peg boards, pin boards, weaving, stick and pea work, sewing, paper folding, chalk and slate work, clay, and tessellations – these offer a variety of activities for helping children to learn. Froebel in Lilley (1967:155) notes:

> Singing, drawing, painting and modelling at an early stage must, therefore, be taken into account in any comprehensive scheme of education. The aim is not to make each pupil proficient in one or all of the arts – though in a sense this is true – nor to turn them all into artists, but to enable every person to develop all sides of his nature, while recognising and appreciating true artistic achievement.

Froebel's philosophy of Early Childhood education is based on four ideas – free self-expression, creativity, social participation and motor expression. Ten years after establishing his school he published his first book, *Education of Man* (1826). Froebel was invited to open schools in Switzerland in 1831, where he stayed for five years. In 1837, he relocated to Bad Blankenburg in Germany and opened the "play and activity institute", coining the term kindergarten three years later. In 1849, Froebel began the first training college for women kindergarten teachers. Froebel in Lilley (1967:53) states that the "structure of play needs to be known by adults if it is to be used for educational purposes". Froebel believes that the learning of infants and young children should be focused around play and their interests. He notes that "a child's play is his work ... because the child learns easily through play it must not be left to chance but has to be an integral part of the curriculum". He also believes that observation of infants from birth is important, again in Lilley (1967:75): "The feeling with which a child is first welcomed should surround him always and should lead to careful observation of the way in which he develops and expresses his thought." He considered observation of children's self-activity to be a fundamental part of practice.

However, Froebel felt an important contribution to Early Childhood education is that of the *Mother Songs*, a book containing 50 songs, each providing guidance for parents on exercises to do with children, plus a symbolic introduction to the abstract values in life. Each song is printed on one page surrounded by pictures illustrating the song in different ways. A pair of hands at the top of the page shows the hand or finger exercise which accompanies the song. In essence, Froebel aims to introduce physical play between mother and child, knowledge about the surrounding world and symbolic meanings of life.

He also recognises the central role of children's first-hand experience, as well as play, families, communication and language; understanding that children are mutually symbol producers and symbol users; their need for movement; and engagement with nature and outdoor learning (Bruce, 2011). Froebel also understands the importance of allowing children the freedom to discover things for themselves and not to discourage them from doing something – even if adults think that it might not be safe, such as climbing trees.

Bruce (1987, 2011) articulates the Froebelian principles as:

- Childhood is part of life, and not simply preparation for it
- The whole child is considered to be important. Health – physical and mental – is emphasised as well as the importance of feelings, relationships, thinking and spiritual aspects
- Learning is not compartmentalised, for everything links
- Intrinsic motivation, resulting in child-initiated and self-directed activity, is valued
- Self-discipline is emphasised
- There are especially receptive periods of learning and sequences of development
- What children can do (rather than what they cannot do) is the starting point for the child's education
- There is an inner life of the child, which emerges under favourable conditions, such as pretending and imagination through play
- The people (both adults and children) with whom the child interacts are of central importance
- The child's education is seen as an interaction between the child and the environment, including the physical, material, other people and knowledge itself

These principles are universal and can be applied to any curriculum framework that supports holistic development and learning.

Susan Isaacs' contribution to Early Childhood education

In 1924, aged 38, Susan Isaacs replied to an advert in the *New Statesman* for a teacher/researcher. Geoffrey Pyke, a wealthy businessman of the day, had placed the advertisement as he wanted to open a school for his son to attend which was free from rules and one that ensured children were learning in a natural environment. Isaacs (1885–1948), an infant teacher, researcher and trained psychoanalyst, was appointed to run the Malting House School in Cambridge, from 1924–1927. Influenced by Froebel's theory on active learning and John Dewey's (1859–1952) emphasis on social interaction, Isaacs believed a natural environment to be the starting point of any child's education.

Susan Isaacs was one of the first educators to use psychoanalytic methods of observation and theoretical analysis in nursery education. Her progressive and modern ideas could be described as being ahead of her time. Her major contribution to Early Years education is a systematic and methodical record-keeping system for gathering qualitative and naturalistic data about children's development. Her psychoanalytic background deeply influenced the observational techniques that underpin much of her work (Graham, 2009). Isaacs' (1952:70) theory is based on three principles – attention to details, observation of context and study of genetic continuity. One of her techniques was to present her staff with the observations of children separately from her analysis and interpretations of each child's social development or intellectual growth. This provided her staff with an opportunity and permission to tap into their values and beliefs and to consider their own interpretation before reading and discussing Isaacs' thoughts. Along with her team, Isaacs (1933:5) tried to capture the entire behaviour of the children. The following ongoing observations by Isaacs (1930:182–183), carried out over three days, capture the children's social and cognitive development, particularly illuminating their continuous learning and how the past affects the children's current interests and preoccupations.

> 13.07.25: *Some of the children call out that the rabbit was ill and dying. They found it in the summer-house, hardly able to move. They were very sorry and talked much about it. They shut it up in the hutch and gave it warm milk. Throughout the morning they kept looking at it; they thought it was getting better, and said it was "not dying to-day".*
>
> 14.07.25: *The rabbit had died in the night. Dan found it and said, "It's dead – its tummy does not move up and down now." Paul said, "My daddy says that*

> if we put it into water, it will get alive again." Mrs I said, "Shall we do so and see?" They put it into a bath of water. Some of them said, "It's alive." Duncan said, "If it floats, it's dead, and if it sinks, it's alive." It floated on the surface. One of them said, "It's alive, because it is moving." This was a circular movement, due to the currents in the water. Mrs I therefore put in a small stick, which also moved round and round, and they agreed that the stick was not alive. They then suggested that they should bury the rabbit, and all helped to dig a hole and bury it. Later on, seeing the puppy lying on the grass in the sun, Duncan called out for fun, "Oh, the puppy is dead!" All the children went to see it and laughed heartily when the puppy got up and ran at them.
>
> 15.07.25: Frank and Duncan talked of digging the rabbit up, but Frank said, "It's not there – it's gone, it's up in the sky." They began to dig, but tired of it, and ran off to something else. Later, they came back, and dug again. Duncan, however, said, "Don't bother – it's gone, it's up in the sky" and gave up digging. Mrs I therefore said, "Shall we see if it is there?" and also dug. They found the rabbit and were very interested to see it still there. Duncan said, "Shall we cut its head off?" They reburied it.

The sheer breadth and depth of Isaacs' observations provide a fascinating and compelling insight into children's never-ending quest to make sense of their world (Abbott & Nutbrown, 2001). For this reason, her work resonates well with the types of ongoing observations that practitioners are expected to gather, based on their firsthand study of young children in action. Over time these create continuous formative observations, revealing children's thoughts and feelings. Many of Isaacs' theoretical methods of observation and data analysis in a child-centred approach have become embedded in the foundations of Early Childhood education (Drummond, 2003; Nutbrown, 2011).

The Malting House School

An underlying principle of the experimental school at which she was employed was to allow children freedom to use their playthings in their own way – much value was placed on play that was free and based on the child's own interpretation of his or her experience. However, Isaacs was deeply interested in how children apply knowledge that they already possess to new situations. Her main interest was in the analysis of children's scientific thinking and understanding. Drawing from a range of methodologies and disciplinary approaches, which included clinical studies and analytic techniques, she pioneered a child-centred approach on engaging with children. Isaacs meticulously recorded the details of children's investigations, explorations, trials and errors and analysed how they showed their feelings, expressed themselves, followed through on their own interests and questioned the what, why and how in all aspects of their development. Isaacs used Freud's term "super-ego" to stand for the uncompromising need for self-expression displayed by the children in her care. In an attempt to understand the whole child, her work focused on observing children in group care situations, made over time and in a range of contexts, using a theoretical frame she devised (1930:52) to help classify her observations.

1. Application of knowledge
A.1. Formal and theoretical application
2. Imaginative and hypothetical application
3. Make-believe and dramatised knowledge
4. Comparisons and analogies
B. Practical insight and resources
11. Increase of knowledge: problems and experiment, observation and discovery
111. Social interchanges of knowledge
A. "Whys", "becauses" and other logical questions and reasoning
B. Discussions: corrections and self-corrections
1V. Miscellaneous

Isaacs recognises that these broad types of cognitive activity overlap – that many of her formative observations are difficult to assign to any one form and that this is psychologically significant. Children's cognitive behaviour is not considered as "a set of single unit acts of relation-findings, but as a complex series of adaptive reactions and reflections".

Through her detailed observational notes, she builds up a picture of the whole child and shows a thorough acknowledgement of the importance of the emotional and social development of each individual. Cognitive development also becomes an important factor in her work. Her observational work is illustrated in two books – *Intellectual Growth in Young Children* (1930) and *Social Development in Young Children* (1933). Her work is systematic and methodical and explores children's relationships with their peers and adults, their emotional, social, physical and intellectual development, their interests and attitudes to learning, and their skills and understanding. Their individual ability to solve problems independently in their play is also evident throughout her writing. For Isaacs, observations of what children can do are the key to understanding the connections and complexities in their spontaneous play and explorations. She draws on the theories of Freud and Klein to explain, critique and give further details about her work. *Social Development in Young Children* draws heavily upon the theories of Klein, with whom she shared a flat. According to Isaacs (1933:410), the educator "must be a 'good' parent to the child, even though she be a strict one".

In a pamphlet to parents, Isaacs (1954:30) describes the role of the adult as being crucial to learning, saying:

Children need not only the right play materials, but skilled help in their own efforts to learn and understand, and in their struggles with anti-social impulses. To know what is the right word to say to the shy or inhibited child, the angry and destructive child, to have the right answer ready to an intellectual problem, to see when to introduce the child to a new piece of number apparatus, to understand when to interfere and when to leave alone, when to check defiance or stop a quarrel, and when to allow the child to solve his own problem, when to encourage and when to remain silent, it is not wisdom that comes simply by nature.

The integration of Isaacs' (1933) educational theory with psychoanalytic theory has also influenced our thinking, particularly because her systematic observations reveal that children's capacities are much greater than had been previously thought. Isaacs' (1930) radical approach to educating children in The Malting House School draws heavily on her psychoanalytical background and deeply influences her theories on the social and emotional behaviour of young children.

Jean Piaget's contributions to Early Childhood education

Jean Piaget (1896–1980) was originally a biologist but became interested in psychology. While working in Paris, administering reading tests on children and measuring their intellectual development, he began to develop theories of child development, leading him into the field of child psychology. In Piaget's writing, his main interest is in children's intellectual development, specifically in the concepts that constitute the building blocks of thinking. Piaget (1977) says: "My central aim has always been to search for the mechanisms of biological adaptation and the analysis and epistemological interpretation of that higher form of adaptation which manifests itself as scientific thought."

The concept of cognitive structure is central to his theory, with much of his research based on observations of his three children, from birth to language. Piaget identifies the stages of intellectual development and describes them as sensory motor (0–18 months), pre-operational (18 months to 7 years) and concrete operational and formal operation (12 years to adulthood). Piaget believes that as humans mature, they go through definite stages of cognitive development. The sequence is fixed, all children go through it in the same order and no stage can be skipped. He calls this the Invariant sequence. Piaget's greatest contribution to Early Years education is that he identifies patterns of repeated actions in children and calls them "schemas", which he defines as "co-ordinated systems of movement and perceptions, which constitute any elementary behaviour capable of being repeated and applied to new situations, e.g., grasping, moving, shaking an object".

Piaget (Piaget & Inhelder, 1969) believes that cognitive structures develop through a process of adaptation, assimilation and accommodation during all development stages. The child experiences his or her environment using whatever mental maps they have constructed so far. If the experience is a repeated one, it fits easily into the child's cognitive structure so that he or she maintains mental equilibrium. However, if the experience is different or new, the child alters his or her cognitive structure to accommodate the new information. In Piaget's schema theory, schemas are identified as functioning at four levels – sensory motor, symbolic representation, functional dependency and abstract thought. Adaptation has two elements to it, assimilation and accommodation. Assimilation is when babies take in new information which they then apply to the schema that they already have, for example, a baby may grasp things in its hands during the sensory motor level. Accommodation is when the baby then modifies his or her behaviour based on new information as they come into contact with objects that are non-graspable. These repeated movements or actions become mental representations, or schemas, that will help the baby to deal with objects and situations. The adaptation process is critical as it enables children to take on new information, form and change ideas, and adopt new behaviours. The adaptation process can occur during the four levels of functioning.

In his work, Piaget describes schemas as being operational and taking place in developing the mind. He argues that children combine these and use them in a logical way. He introduces the notion of equilibrium as mental organisation that keeps a balance between assimilation and accommodation. He believes that if something new happens for which the child does not have a schema, the child's existing schema must be accommodated and adapted to take in the new information. As a result, new interconnections are made and the child, through play, can test out new ideas and concepts. According to Piaget's theory, each time the child accommodates a new event or problem, intellectual growth is nudged closer to maturity as a result of changing ideas about the world and generating more adaptive schemas. Piaget maintains that children erect more and more adequate structures – he views the child as an active learner and believes that knowledge should not merely be verbally transmitted but must be constructed and reconstructed by the learner. Piaget asserts that for a child to know and construct knowledge of the world, the child must act on objects and it is this which provides knowledge of objects.

Piaget (Piaget & Inhelder, 1969: 95) does not view language development as a major aspect of overall development in the child. He believes that early speech, like early thought is egocentric, meaning that the child is centred on self and ignores what others have to say. He implies that language does not affect thought – thought determines language. According to Piaget (Piaget & Inhelder, 1969:128), words used by 2–4-year-olds do not express what he calls "concept", but rather "pre-concepts". But in order to think at an abstract level he does see language as being of central importance. He states: "It is not yet a logical concept and is still partly something of a pattern of action and of sensory motor assimilation." For Piaget, language is a system for representing the world and is quite separate from actions, which form the process of reasoning or logic.

Piaget believes that during this stage the child has started to represent things symbolically and describes the function of symbolic play as to "satisfy the self by transforming what is real into what is desired". He proposes that children's ideas and concepts are initially a result of physical experience so that before children can comprehend and manipulate symbols in reading, mathematics and writing, for example, they first need concrete opportunities to encounter real objects or events which the symbols stand for.

Lev Vygotsky's contribution to Early Childhood education

Lev Semyonovich Vygotsky (1896–1934) was an important Russian psychologist. In 1913, he entered Moscow University to study poetry and philosophy but soon changed to law. Later, Vygotsky taught literature at a provincial school where he began to give lectures on psychology. Influenced by Marxist-Leninist theory, Vygotsky developed his own theory and was put under pressure to adapt it to the then Soviet Union's political ideology. Due to many different factors, including those related to the particular political relationship between the United States and the Soviet Union, Vygotsky's work was unknown in the West for many decades. When the Cold War ended, the incredible wealth of Vygotsky's work started to emerge. Vygotsky's work was published after the death of Susan Isaacs.

Vygotsky emphasises the links between social factors of culture and historical nature and those of a more interpersonal nature. He considers the determining factor of a child's psychological development to be social development, especially language development. Vygotsky (1978:46) developed theories that implicitly emphasise the social and cultural aspects of the biological learning process. He states:

> Within a general process of development, two qualitatively different lines of development, differing in origin, can be distinguished: the elementary processes, which are of biological origin, on the one hand, and the higher psychological functions, of sociocultural origin, on the other. The history of child behaviour is born from the interweaving of these two lines.

Learning, according to Vygotsky, depends on development, but development is not dependent on learning. Development can be furthered by effective instructions. Vygotsky believes that learning is shaped by social and cultural interactions – interactions and traditions can only be understood in the context of, or with reference to, this same cultural and historical context. Vygotsky (1978:56) explains how children's basic actions become a gesture or sign with meaning, shared between people. Pointing begins as "an unsuccessful attempt to grasp something, a mere movement towards an object". Vygotsky believes that the development of children's higher mental functions is a product of their interactions with more accomplished members of their culture, such as parents, educators, siblings and peers. Through interaction with more capable members of a society, the child is aided to realise his or her movements towards the object. Vygotsky believes that this is not an image of a child on its own solving problems, there is a relationship between the adult, child and environment. When an adult comes to the child's aid and understands that the child's movements indicate something, the meaning of the grasping movements becomes recognised by others. According to Vygotsky (1978:57), children's cognitive development is derived "first between people (inter-psychological), and then inside the child (intra-psychological), as it is socially and culturally constructed, and then internalised". He argues that learning is both a social and cultural experience and what adults (who are cultural tools) do, think and say in their interactions with children will determine how they construct and transform their new and existing knowledge to make sense of the world.

Language and thought

The origins of thought and language, according to Vygotsky, are that thought and speech have different roots in humankind – thought being non-verbal and language being non-intellectual at an early stage. But the development lines are not parallel; they cross again and again. Vygotsky (1934/1986:219) states:

> The structure of speech does not simply mirror the structure of thought; that is why words cannot be put on by thought like a ready-made garment. Thought undergoes many changes as it turns into speech. It does not merely find expression in speech; it finds its reality and form.

He believes that at a certain moment, around the age of two, the curves of development of thought and speech – until then separate – meet and join to initiate a new form of behaviour. This is when thought becomes verbal and speech becomes rational. Vygotsky says that when children reach the age of about 4, the language itself helps the child to form ideas and the child is able to describe both what he or she is doing, and what they are going to do. He calls this "inner speech". The purpose of inner speech, according to Vygotsky, is to control, plan, recall and predict.

Vygotsky believes that language is not only a cognitive tool for communication. He identifies the use of the symbol system as being a product of human beings, developed in various ways by different and diverse cultures over time. Vygotsky (1978:108) states: "For children some objects can readily denote others, replacing them and becoming signs for them, and the degree of similarity between a plaything and the object it denotes is unimportant." What is most important is the utilisation of the plaything and the possibility of executing a representational gesture with it. This is key to the entire symbolic function of children's play. Vygotsky (1978:108) says: "From this point of view, therefore, children's symbolic play can be understood as a very complex system of 'speech' through gestures that communicate and indicate the meaning of playthings." Because Vygotsky considers the determining factor in a child's psychological development to be social development, especially language development embodied in symbolic function of gesture, play and speech, he maintains that symbolism is an important characteristic of human activity that is imposed on an individual's behaviour, shaping it and reconstructing it along the lines of a social-cultural matrix. Vygotsky (1978:97) believes that once children begin to use one thing to stand in for another, they begin to understand the symbolic function of language. He says: "In play, thought is separated from objects and action arises from ideas rather than from things: a piece of wood begins to be a doll and a stick becomes a horse."

For Vygotsky, a clear knowledge of the interrelations between thought and language is necessary for understanding children's intellectual development. In this he includes cultural artefacts which affect the child in everyday life. He suggests that language is not merely an expression of the knowledge that the child has acquired but there is a fundamental correspondence between thought and speech, in terms of one providing a resource for the other.

Vygotsky (1978) identifies the Zone of Proximal Development (ZPD) as the difference between children's ability to solve a problem alone and their ability to solve problems with adult support. Central to this theory is the notion that adults can stimulate the process of learning by participating in cultural activities and giving children the required help and appropriate level of support in culturally relevant ways. He holds that "good learning" is that which is in advance of development and creates a new ZPD. The role of the adult in supporting current and future learning can therefore be defined by their knowledge about the stage of development of individual children – not only knowing what has already been achieved but also what a child will need in the course of "maturing" (ibid:87).

Vygotsky (1978, 1981), Bronfenbrenner (1979) and Bruner (1986) consider the role of the adult to be one that engages a child through interaction and dialogue: the child is viewed as an active and constructive learner in a socially mediated process that is dependent on the support of an adult. According to Vygotsky (1991:17): "The child must act himself; the teacher should only manage and guide this activity."

Comparisons and contrasts about how children learn

Friedrich Froebel (1885), Susan Isaacs (1930), Jean Piaget (1926) and Lev Vygotsky (1978) all start out with the same basic views of the child as a biological organism. Between them, they provide us with many ideas old and new. There are many similarities in their methodological approaches, such as systematic observations of natural behaviour to discover underlying thought and emotional and socio-cultural processes. Froebel and Piaget place much emphasis on children learning through their senses. Froebel and Isaacs provide important support for the education of young children, taking the focus off rote learning of books and onto observing children. They all place great importance on the study of scientific concepts in the child. However, Froebel, Isaacs and Vygotsky place much more emphasis on the study of children under particular conditions, whereas, although Piaget observed his own children in the home context, he later, when working in the Binet laboratories, carried out experiments. Isaacs (1933:4) states that the underlying principle for gathering qualitative and naturalistic data, rather than carrying out experiments, is that:

> experimental methods have in fact proved enormously fruitful in the study of intellectual growth, of learning and of language. But in the field of social development they are almost inapplicable. To study the moral development of children by asking for their judgements at different ages on a series of fables or of moral situations, for example, is to consider only one very limited aspect of the problem ... we can only study their effective morality in its spontaneous action in real situations.

Piaget's (1926) theory has been very influential in our understanding about how children acquire knowledge. Isaacs (1930), Vygotsky (1978), Karmiloff-Smith (1979) and Donaldson (1978) have all been critical of aspects of Piaget's experimental technique. Isaacs asserts his stages of intellectual development are merely typical, rather than set in stone. She (1930:44) used her systematic observations to explain that many of the children at The Malting House School could function at much higher levels than Piaget's research on the ages and stages of intellectual development originally suggests. Isaacs (1930:73) also critiques his theory for being complex and elaborate. She states: "He offers us a highly articulated and elaborated picture of the development of the child, rather than a series of studies of particular children under particular conditions." Vygotsky (1978:78–79) writes, as part of a review and critique of Piaget's work, that he fails to explicitly guide the interplay between the child's relationships and reality. Piaget's theory, he says, contains an apparent weakness that is illuminated by the observational work of Isaacs and can be viewed as both rigid and narrow, specifically since the complexity and richness of intellectual development cannot be contained within his four stages. However, Isaacs (1930) and Vygotsky (1978) both find that children are able to do things far earlier than Piaget had predicated. The social and cultural theories introduced by Vygotsky show how children learn through interaction with more knowledgeable others, symbolic play and other forms of play. Isaacs' detailed observations of children's play provide further evidence to support the notion that play is central to developing learning.

In their theories on mental growth, Vygotsky and Piaget refer to internalisation and emphasise the necessity of a developmental approach, in which active learning is central to both learning and discovery. Vygotsky and Piaget also provide useful insights into how children develop. The observations of Froebel (1885) and Isaacs (1930) capture the whole child's emotional, social and cognitive development under child-centred free play conditions. Piaget focuses on what it is within the organism that leads to cognitive change. Vygotsky (1978) is interested in activity as a social phenomenon, exploring how social experience might cause important revisions in the child's thinking. Froebel (1885), Isaacs (1930) and Vygotsky (1978) assert that the role of the adult is an important feature in similar ways but in a different cultural context. Froebel talks about the adult providing children with freedom and guidance – this means to continually watch children passively while internally trying to make sense of what is being observed. Froebel also suggests it is the role of the adult to carefully structure the learning environment in order to facilitate learning. For Isaacs, the adult role is to provide consistent boundaries and guidance, similar to Froebel, whereas for Vygotsky it is the idea of cooperation, learning through the Zone of Proximal Development. Piaget accepts the notion that members of the child's culture can aid development through instruction and dialogue, although not in the radically transforming way that Vygotsky proposes. For Piaget, instruction can refine and improve structures that have already emerged, but it cannot lead to development of concepts as Vygotsky thinks it does. Because Froebel (1885), Isaacs (1930), Piaget (1959) and Vygotsky (1978) share a set of basic beliefs about development, their theories are best viewed not in opposition to one another, but as complementary.

Sigmund Freud

The foundation stone of child analysis is the work of Sigmund Freud. In 1909, he published *Analysis of a Phobia in a Five-Year-Old Boy*, known as Little Hans. Freud used case studies to inform his theory on psychoanalysis. However, he kept poor notes and records and did not present systematic objective observations. Although Freud drew important conclusions about the case, he made no further systematic study of children.

Freud (1923) is interested in the structure of the mind. He divides mental life into three entities – the "id", the "ego" and the "super-ego" – and he views mental life as one which proceeds on conscious and unconscious levels. He believes that the id is mainly unconscious and primitive, thus creating the first form of thought and urges. The ego, according to Freud (1923), develops between the ages of 2 and 3 years and is the part of the mind which forces the id to remain in touch with reality, being ruled by what people and society expect. The third part of the mind, the super-ego, develops from around 5 years of age, and tries to gratify urges within the limits of society and reality. Freud believes that all these parts constantly interact with each other, though each has its own separate and distinct goal. It is this factor which incites the internal conflict seen in humans. In this model, conflict occurs when the id interacts with the super-ego, and the ego bears the responsibility for negotiating between these two extremes. For Freud, humans are therefore in constant conflict with themselves; torn between their animal nature and their ideas of a culture that internalises the values of one's parents. This belief system is fundamental to Freud's preoccupation with uncovering the unconscious mind, which led to the development of his four techniques of "free association", "dream analysis", "projective techniques" and "recovered memories". The chief aim of each of these is to uncover the unconscious mind.

Anna Freud

Freud's daughter Anna, also a psychoanalyst, continued the work of her father after his death in 1939, developing his theories on "defence mechanisms" and "separation and attachment". Anna Freud (1936) was interested in the whole child – how the child develops emotionally, intellectually, educationally, physically and psychologically, in relation to family and friends. In 1941, she set up the Hampstead War Nurseries, an institution that provided foster care for 80 single-parent families during the Second World War. Her aim was to help the children form attachments to their new carers by providing consistent relationships with the helpers. To achieve this end, she had to encourage the perseverance of the mothers throughout the project. This undertaking was to prove critical, leading Anna Freud to a conscious awareness of the very real impact and effect that deprivation and trauma can have on young children. In her analysis, children go through several stages of normal psychological development and these stages can be seen through observation. Making diagnostic profiles of six stages of development using developmental growth charts enabled Anna Freud (1975) to separate and identify specific factors that deviate from normal development and define the pattern of inter-relational egocentricity to objectivity. She believes that children move through phases of play from isolation to becoming increasingly cooperative, though remaining self-reliant. This is then followed by an ability to become more accommodating to others. Gardner (1969:169) argues that this conveys the relevance of the contributions that educational theorists such as Froebel, Isaacs, Dewey, Piaget, Montessori and Freud made to Early Childhood education; she believes that they provided practitioners with a bridge with which to link principles to practice.

Anna Freud (1936) acknowledges the huge variations in child development but, unlike Piaget and Inhelder (1969), she does not apply developmental ages to her identified stages. Although it does not mention Anna Freud by name when discussing the subject of children's infantile projections of their thoughts and wishes onto others in the nursery classroom, the Plowden Report (1967:17) formally endorses psychoanalytic concepts in nursery education. It says:

> The persistence of early responses, and particularly of unconscious emotional attitudes towards other people, has been stressed especially by the psychoanalysts. Children 'identify' with parents and others, imitate them and assume their attitudes. They also project onto them many of their own infantile thoughts and wishes. As they grow up, they may transfer these attitudes to others in their environment. Thus, the child may re-enact this parental relationship with his teacher; a teacher may partly re-enact with colleagues his own earlier relationships with parents or siblings. Such identification, and the formation of strong emotional bonds between child and teacher, can be valuable educationally if the bonds are positive ones.

Anna Freud's work is significant and important because it underpins the psychoanalytic principles in which the concepts of projection, containment and transference and counter transference are brought to the surface by sensitive observations.

Other post-Freudian theorists, such as Melanie Klein et al. (1952), also extended and expanded on the work of Freud. Klein developed the concept of "an unconscious inner world in humans" based on the belief that children would express their fears and feelings through playing with toys. After the war, she developed the technique of "play therapy", which attempts to reveal children's unconscious motivations, showing how these affect a child's developing ego, super-ego and sexuality. Play therapy is substituted for Sigmund Freud's "free association", the technique that encapsulates his view that young children are incapable of censoring their own thoughts. This caused a major rift in the psychoanalytic community, with many taking sides or breaking away. Anna Freud holds a similar view to her father, arguing that infants cannot be analysed as early as Klein claims, as they do have enough first-hand experiences to draw from. This caused yet another division in the Psychoanalytic Society, resulting in Susan Isaacs siding with Klein.

Psychoanalytic concepts

Psychoanalytic concepts of projection, containment and holding are still central to theoretical considerations about understanding the whole child. Developed by Bion (1962), the idea of the contained and the container refers to a person (the practitioner) being able to contain the distressed feelings demonstrated by the child, later returning them to the child once they are no longer anxious or upset. According to Bion (1962:90):

> Container and contained are susceptible of conjunction and permeation by emotion. Thus conjoined or permeated, or both, they change in a manner usually described as growth. When disjoined or denuded of emotion they diminish in vitality, that is, approximate, to inanimate objects. Both the container and the contained are models of abstract representations of psychoanalytic realisations.

This approach, however, relies heavily on practitioners acknowledging their emotional links with the child, and on the idea that the person (the practitioner), acting as the container, must know what feelings are coming from the child, and what feelings belong to them.

The concept of "holding" was developed by Winnicott (1960:49), defined as "the physical holding of the infant which is a form of loving". It is perhaps the main way in which a mother can show the infant her love. There are those who can "hold" an infant and those who cannot; the latter quickly producing a sense of insecurity and distressed crying. For Winnicott (1965/2006), "holding" includes the actual physical holding of a child, but also the psychological holding, where the person (the practitioner) can respond appropriately to the child's social and emotional struggles. Although the psychoanalytic concept of "containment" is similar to the concept of "holding", Winnicott (1965/2006) disagrees with Bion (1962) about the capacity of the infant to project unmanageably distressed feelings onto the carer.

Isaacs' pioneering approach, which relates directly to how practitioners analyse development and learning and the need to systematically record children's experiences in detail, has been omitted from the policy discourse. Early Years educators are required to observe children carefully and record what they see, but mere observation implies the attentive watching of a child. What is problematic here is that educators who take part in the actual assessments often do not understand the significance of what has been observed and how it should best inform next steps.

Conclusion

The influence of Froebel, Isaacs, Vygotsky, Piaget, Bion, Winnicott, Freud and others mentioned in this chapter have all contributed to the theory and practice of Early Childhood education, by adding to our understanding of child development. Bruce (2001:19) reminds us that child development theories help us to "predict and anticipate how children might behave". Indeed, all of these theories help us to make sense of children's play and explorations that we see. They can also help us to analyse and interpret play and tune into developing learning – linking what we have observed with what they have found. Sometimes our observations will fit nicely into these theories and sometimes they will not. What is important here is that these theories help us to think much more deeply about children's developing learning and their work remains alive today.

In the next chapter we turn our attention to the role of the educator – observing, interpreting and supporting children's development.

Bibliography

Abbott, L. & Nutbrown, C. (2001) *Experiencing Reggio Emilia: Implications for Preschool Provision*. Buckingham, PA: Open University Press.

Bion, W. (1962) *Learning through Experience*. London: Heinemann.

Bronfenbrenner, U. (1979) *The Ecology of Human Development*. Cambridge, MA: Harvard University Press.

Bronfenbrenner, U. (1992) 'Ecological Systems Theory'. In: Vasta, R. (ed) *Six Theories of Child Development: Revised Formulations and Current Issues*. pp. 187–249. London: Jessica Kingsley.

Bruce, T. (1987) *Early Childhood Education*. London, Sydney: Hodder and Stoughton.

Bruce, T. (2001) *Learning through Play: Babies, and Toddlers and the Foundation Years*. London: Hodder and Stoughton.

Bruce, T. (2011) *Early Childhood Education*. 4th edn. London: Hodder and Stoughton.

Bruner, J. S. (1960) *The Process of Education*. Cambridge, MA: Harvard University Press.

Bruner, J. S. (1986) *Actual Minds, Possible Worlds*. Cambridge, MA: Harvard University Press.

Bruner, J. S. (1990) *Acts of Meaning*. Cambridge, MA: Harvard University Press.

Department of Education and Science. (1990) *Starting with Quality: Report of the Committee of Enquiry into the Quality of Education Experience Offered to Three-and-Four-Year-Olds*. Rumbold Report. HMSO, London.

Dewey, J. (1963) *Experience and Education*. New York: First Collier Books Macmillan Publishing Co.

Donaldson, M. (1978) *Children's Minds*. London: Collins/Fontana.

Drummond, M. J. (2003) *Assessing Children's Learning*. 2nd edn. London: David Fulton Publishers.

Fleer, M. & Richardson, C. (2004) 'Mapping the Transformation of Understanding'. In: Anning, A., Cullen, J., & Fleer, M. (eds) *Early Childhood Education*. pp. 130–144. London, Thousand Oaks, CA, New Delhi: Sage.

Fleer, M. & Robbins, J. (2007) 'A Cultural-Historical Analysis of Early Childhood Education: How Do Teachers Appropriate New Cultural Tools?'. *European Early Childhood Research Journal*. 15 (1) pp. 103–119.

Freud, A. (1936) *The Writings of Anna Freud, Volume II, 1936: The Ego and the Mechanisms of Defense*. New York: International Universities Press.

Freud, A. (1975) *Introduction to the Technique of Child Analysis*. Stratford NH: Ayer Co Publishing.

Freud, S. (1923) *The Ego and the Id*. London: Hogarth.

Froebel, F. (1826) *The Education of Man*, New York and London: D. Appleton and Company.

Froebel, F. (1885) *The Education of Man*. [trans. Jarvis, J]. New York: A. Lovell & Company.

Froebel, F. (1887) *The Education of Man*. New York: Appleton.

Froebel, F. (1895) *The Mottoes and Commentaries of Friedrich Froebel's Mother Play*. [trans. H.R. Eliot & S.E. Blow]. New York: D. Appleton & Company, 1902.

Froebel, F. (1899) *Education by Development: The Second Part of the Pedagogics of the Kindergarten* [trans. Jarvis, J]. Reprint. New York: D. Appleton & Company.

Gallach, L. (2006) *Block Play, the Sand Pit and the Doll Corner: The (Dis)ordering Materialities of Educating Young Children*. Online papers archived by the Institute of Geography, School of Geosciences, University of Edinburgh, Edinburgh.

Gardner, D. (1969) *Susan Isaacs; the First Biography*. London: Methuen Education Limited.

Graham, P. (2009) *Susan Isaacs: A Life Freeing the Mind of Children*. London: Karnac.

Isaacs, S. (1930) *Intellectual Growth in Young Children*. New York: Harcourt.

Isaacs, S. (1933) *Social Development in Young Children*. New York: Harcourt.

Isaacs, S. (1952) *The Educational Value of the Nursery School*. London: Headly Brothers Ltd.

Isaacs, S. (1954) *The Educational Value of the Nursery School*. London: BAECE – Early Education.

Isaacs, S. (1968) *The Nursery Years*. London: Routledge and Kegan Paul.

Karmiloff-Smith, A. (1979) *A Functional Approach to Child Language*. Cambridge University Press: Cambridge, UK.

Klein, M., Heimann, P., Isaacs, S., & Riviere, J. (1952) *Developments in Psychoanalysis*. London: Hogarth.

Lilley, I. M. (1967) *Friedrich Froebel. A Selection from His Writing*. Cambridge: Cambridge University Press.

Manning, J. P. (2005) 'Rediscovering Froebel: A Call to Examine His Life and Gifts'. *Early Childhood Education Journal*. 32 (6) pp. 371–376.

Nawrotzki, K. (2006) 'Froebel Is Dead; Long Live Froebel! the National Froebel Foundation and English Education'. *History of Education: Journal of the History of Education Society*. 35 (2) pp. 209–271.

Nutbrown, C. (2011) *Threads of Thinking. Schemas and Young Children's Learning* (4th ed.) London: Sage.

Piaget, J. (1959) *The language and thought of the child* (3rd ed.) London: Routledge.

Piaget, J. (1926) *The Language and Thought of the Child*. London: Routledge & Kengan Paul.

Piaget, J. (1977) 'Problems of Equilibration'. In: Appel, M. H. & Goldbery, L. S. (eds) *Topics in Cognitive Development – Vol. 1 Equilibration: Theory, Research, and Application*. pp. 3–13. New York: Plenum.

Piaget, J. & Inhelder, B. (1969) *The Psychology of the Child*. London: Routledge & Kegan Paul.

Quinn, S. F. (2013) 'Froebel's Gifts'. www.froebel.org.uk.

The Plowden Report. (1967) *Children And Their Primary Schools*. London: HMSO

Tovey, H. (2013) *Bringing the Froebel Approach to Your Early Years Practice*. Abingdon: Routledge.

Tovey, H. (2018) 'Friedrich Froebel, His Life and His Ideas'. In: Bruce, T., Elfer, P., & Powell, S. (eds) *The Routledge International Handbook of Froebel and Early Childhood Practice: Re-articulating Research and Policy*. pp. 7–13. Abingdon: Routledge.

Vygotsky, L. S. (1934/1986) *Thought and Language* [ed. Kozulin, A.]. Cambridge: MA: MIT Press.

Vygotsky, L. S. (1978) *Mind and Society: The Development of Higher Mental Processes*. Cambridge, MA: Harvard University Press.

Vygotsky, L. S. (1981) 'The Genesis of Higher Mental Functions'. In: Wertsch, J. V. (ed) *The Concept of Activity in Soviet Psychology*. pp. 144–188. Armonk, NY: M.E. Sharpe.

Vygotsky, L. (1991) in Davydov (1995) *The Influence of L. S. Vygotsky on Education Theory, Research, and Practice. Educational Researcher*, 24 (3) pp. 12–21

Vygotsky, L. S. (1997) 'The History of the Development of Higher Mental Functions'. In: Rieber, R. W., and Hall, M. J. (eds) *The Collected Works of L.S. Vygotsky, Vol. 4*. pp. 153–179. New York: Plenum.

Whinnet, J. (2012) 'Gifts and Occupations – Froebel's Gifts (Wooden Block Play) and Occupations (Construction and Workshop Experiences) Today'. In: Bruce, T. (ed) *Early Childhood Practice: Froebel Today*. pp. 121–136. London: Sage.

Wiggin, K. D. & Smith, N. A. (1900) *Froebel's Occupations*. Boston & New York: Houghton, Mifflin & Co.

Winnicott, D. W. (1960) The theory of the parent-infant relationshi. In: Winnicott, D. W. (ed) *The Maturational Processes and the Facilitating Environment*, pp 37–55. London: Hogarth Press.

Winnicott, D. W. (1965/2006) *The Family and Individual Development*. London: Routledge Classics.

2 | The role of the Early Years educator and observation

Introduction

How Early Years educators observe children's learning through their own efforts is key to supporting its development. However, many educators struggle with the process of observation and may not always know how to support groups or individual children – especially if they do not know how to recognise biological development, implement the curriculum, or understand how play is structured. Observation works best when educators understand that children learn through doing, which leads to thinking, reasoning and understanding. A number of scholars, such as Nutbrown (2012) and Callanan et al. (2017), have shown that a lack of skill in carrying out observations is a major problem, especially among Early Years educators who cannot confidently articulate learning, coupled with a lack of knowledge of child development – as a major problem (Nutbrown, 2012; Callanan et al., 2017). Generally, in practice, a narrow checklist culture exists. The current approach to observing children's development has been identified as an important contributing factor to this (Stephen, 2010) as it tends to view Early Years educators as mere technicians ticking off a list of skills and behaviours that a child is able to perform. Goouch and Powell (2013) consider other factors to be a lack of training and support offered to Early Years educators who work with infants and young children and a failure by policy-makers to recognise the educational value of this work.

Goouch and Powell found that the least qualified staff often work with the babies. So, what reasonable steps should we take to provide support and Continuing Professional Development (CPD) for Early Years educators who are currently working with the youngest and most vulnerable infants and young children? Without training and support to develop understanding of child development and theories, Early Years educators may find the expectations of the observation process to be isolating and tough – especially since interpreting children's play and other developmental behaviour requires more than just surface knowledge of child development. For change to happen in Early Years settings across the world, Early Years educators need to engage with and understand a different paradigm to the one they are presently working with as it relates to observations of child development and learning.

Early Years educators should understand that the child development model they are working with determines and influences the way in which they observe infants and young children, placing boundaries around what they expect to see, what questions they ask, and what answers they accept. These then determine what they observe (Manning-Morton, 2006). The paradigm that we are moving away from involves viewing observations as being made up of sets of technical skills, separate from child development, with the emphasis on observing these skills. The techniques thought to be required for observing children's development, and understanding children's need for exploration, manipulation, practice and repetition, are not well known to Early Years educators. Many do not understand this progression and, as a result, are unable to provide infants and young children with developmentally appropriate activities which support, extend or facilitate development and learning.

The findings of my research into this Work Group Supervision model suggest that Early Years educators need to see child development and learning as a process of continuous testing and learning – not just for the children, but also for themselves. What Early Years educators do with their observations is significant and important. Observing infants and young children involves understanding their needs, relationships and first-hand experiences. These help Early Years educators to understand what infants and young children know and can do.

But how can Early Years educators help children to progress and thrive if they do not have a basic understanding of development and learning? What is their role as an educator if it is not to teach and assess skills? To find solutions, Early Years educators need regular opportunities to examine their own beliefs about development and learning as well as explore other people's perspectives and pedagogical insights (Bruce, Louis & McCall, 2015; Bruce, 2019). They also need to observe and experience good practice to realise that skills can be taught in holistic and meaningful ways.

Introducing the role of the Early Years educator

It is important to note that, by definition, Early Years educators cannot truly be viewed as a homogenous group. The ability to interpret and appropriately scaffold learning is profoundly influenced by training, qualifications, attitudes, experiences, knowledge and skills, and most importantly, their willingness to reflect on their practice, discuss habits, and evaluate their interpersonal skills. These are greatly influenced and affected by factors such as motivation, psychological well-being and emotional health. All of these can have an impact on practice.

The term "Early Years educator" is used to describe adults who work with children under the age of 5 years. Included in this category are teaching professionals who have undertaken a four-year degree course, qualified Early Years educators who have pursued a two-year training course, and unqualified support staff, who come from all walks of life and might have limited access to in-service training. Therefore, the term Early Years educator, in the context of Early Childhood, is used to bring together a wide range of professionals who have varying degrees of pedagogical knowledge relating to child development, teaching and learning. The difficulty with the term is that it conceals the various levels of professional knowledge. Athey (2009:16) notes that generalised terms tend to hide professional aspirations and gains of the past. Bringing to light a practitioner's history of professional knowledge and what they know now is key in helping the researcher identify necessary types of knowledge construction and deconstruction, thereby becoming more able to build on the differences seen in professional interactions.

Typically, the working day of Early Years educators is a busy one. They may need to perform dozens of different duties and interact with several children, each with their own unique demands, including children with special educational needs. Often, they may also be the first point of contact for worried or concerned parents.

Broadly speaking, Early Years educators are involved in:

- Observation, assessment and planning
- Monitoring children's progress
- Understanding children's individual needs
- Supporting learning and development through play-based activities
- Creating a stimulating and enabling learning environment
- Sharing knowledge of how children learn with parents to enable support
- Enabling children to build their physical, social, creative, literacy, language and numeracy skills
- Planning stimulating and developmentally appropriate activities
- Helping children get ready for school
- Supporting children to become independent
- Creating the right balance between adult-led and child-initiated activities

However, the number of Early Years educators able to carry out these duties confidently and effectively remains limited. Even when they hold a professional qualification, many are not yet able to support the holistic development of children's learning experiences. It is recognised that Early Years educators play a crucial role in determining the quality of provision – the better the quality of childcare and early education, the better it is for children's development.

Children need knowledgeable and well-trained adults who understand that they learn best when they are able to follow their own interests and explore their own creativity. Knowledge of child development is pertinent to understanding the child's world and forms part of every aspect of how we get to know them. Having knowledge and understanding about the development of early language and literacy is vital. Dalli (2014) states that "babies and toddlers are learners from birth; sensitive responsive caregiving and emotionally attuned interactions in low stress environments open up their brain for learning". This suggests that the communication environment, for babies and toddlers during the first 24 months influences their language acquisition. Interactions affect brain development and learning and the better they are the better connections the babies will make. Anning and Edwards (1999) note that in Early Years settings, staff working in "care" settings prioritise language development rather than a "school" view of literacy, which teachers tend to put first. Moreover, they point out that teachers' views on literacy are influenced by their background as well as their training. This shows the importance and availability of Continuing Professional Development and training. It also highlights the possibility that teachers' personal history and experience can influence how they view literacy and how they teach it. According to Medwell et al. (1998:6), understanding teachers' beliefs is important when designing professional development programmes which aim to change practice.

The Early Years curriculum

Bruce (1987:3) outlines three main attitudes that are held towards children – Empiricism, Nativism and Interactionism. Empiricism starts with what the child does not know – the role of the adult is to recognise missing concepts, skills and experiences, select appropriate ones, and teach step by step with learning broken down into bits. Nativism maintains that human beings are biologically wired to behave in certain ways. The role of the adult is to offer help but not enforce it by interfering with development and learning. Interactionism involves an amalgamation of Empiricism and Nativism, so that interaction takes place within the child.

Many countries have developed and implemented Early Years curriculums based on a range of concepts of what Early Years education actually is. This then creates a tension between the different approaches and understanding of how infants and young children develop and learn. This tension also reflects on how Early Years educators observe children, which can have an adverse impact on the quality of care and education offered at all levels. Melhuish (2014:35) points out that:

> countries vary enormously in their provision of early childhood education and care (ECEC). Almost every developed country has set up some form of early

childhood education for children below the age of compulsory schooling. The differences lie in the organisational forms, the level of state subsidy, the responsible authorities and the age at which children access provision. In many countries, public authorities offer subsidised places for ECEC from a very early age – often from the end of statutory maternity leave. Yet, even in the most developed countries, the ECEC provided is often of poor or modest quality and not tailored to optimise children's development and well-being. The ECEC provided must be of adequate quality if it is to produce benefits for children.

Chukovsky (1963:136) notes that:

> there are many people today who are incapable of seeing the life of the child as a process, that is, as being in constant flux, change and development. Such people are still under the illusion that a child is merely like a trunk, and that only what is put into it will be found there later. If love for a wolf or a mosquito or a fly is placed in the child's soul it will remain there to the end of his days! And these people try to cram into this 'trunk' as many good things as possible, and they are surprised when they later find in it not all the things they stored there.

A more adult-directed approach has been heavily influenced by Empiricism as a source of curriculum content and methods of teaching. An underlying assumption of this position is that children are empty vessels waiting to be filled and then moulded into shape by the adult. This assumption is questionable, especially as it reflects a deficit model in which testing of skills is central. Nativism supposes that children are pre-programmed to unfold from within in particular directions. A combination of the two recognises interaction within and between these positions.

That said, in many Early Years settings children are expected to do the same thing, at the same time, with the same outcome or product. One example would be all children producing the same coloured-in autumn tree as opposed to children having agency and creativity, representing their own first-hand experience and encounters of autumn as competent learners. Children cannot be made to play. They may go and play where instructed to, but the observer will only see superficial play and not deep-level learning. Children need time to play, or wallow as described by Bruce (1997). Wallowing means a child having time to play, exploring their feelings, ideas and relationships and becoming aware of what they know. It is while they are playing that Early Years educators are expected to observe them in order to find out what they are interested in and what they know and can do. It is critical that Early Years educators understand that children learn best when they can follow their own interests and explore their creativity in meaningful ways. By skilfully observing children, Early Years educators find out how to help them progress.

Observation practice in Early Years settings

The ability to observe is seen as a key and distinguishing characteristic of Early Years educators. In their everyday practice, they are expected to observe, support, extend and deepen children's learning as it develops. Early Years educators will expect to work with individuals and groups of children (including those with additional learning needs) and their families. They are also expected to keep ongoing formative observations on all the children in their group. An ability to recall a sequence of events accurately, and be factual and descriptive, is necessary – essentially having a sound knowledge of child development. Observations help to guide the daily practice of Early Years educators and can be useful when sharing information about children's development and learning with parents and other agencies. An ability to observe, recall, record and write up observations is a very important skill they will be expected to hold.

It is equally important that Early Years educators working with infants and young children have a detailed knowledge of how they develop and learn. Then they would know why children do things at a particular age, what children can and cannot do, and when to offer help. Nutbrown (2012) notes the extent to which Early Years educators' knowledge and understanding of children has declined, and is continuing to decline, in most countries where Early Childhood education has seen an expansion.

Within this diverse workforce, the majority of Early Years educators are women, with relatively low levels of training and pay (Bruce, Elfer & Powell, 2018; Bruce, 2019). Many lack the ability to observe children and have little knowledge of when and how to intervene to support and guide learning as it develops. This has negatively affected numerous Early Years educators, leaving them with a perceived sense of inadequacy and lack of knowledge, skills and confidence. Many do not feel confident in their professional and pedagogical practice. These factors can have an adverse impact on the quality of care and education offered to children at all levels, specifically when misconceptions exist about how young children learn.

Early Years educators entering the profession today also come from a variety of backgrounds and many have not learnt the basics in child development or have opportunities to reflect on the processes of their observations. Under such conditions, what should be done to support the Early Years educator to learn how to observe, and how can Early Years educators ensure that all children are supported to reach their goals?

Many Early Years educators have not had opportunities to discover the centrality of play in stimulating and coordinating development and learning. Currently, the Empiricism view of child development prevails through assessments and baseline tests. These tests do not involve observing children in a context that is meaningful to them, nor do they acknowledge young children as active learners intent on making sense of the world around them. This then leads to decontextualised teaching methods at odds with well-established research understandings of the holistic nature of development and learning. These underserve infants and young children. If Early Years educators are to acquire a deep understanding of children in early childhood, they must learn to observe them and examine these observations closely, so that they can assess the children's needs and plan ways to help them, based on what they know about the children they are observing. Learning how to effectively observe children is a very important skill. With this knowledge and understanding, Early Years educators are more able to support, extend and deepen learning experiences.

Child development: Learning in infants and young children

How can Early Years educators recognise children's development and learning if they do not understand what they are seeing? This question forces us to think about what we take notice of when we observe. Knowing what information children are gathering and learning while they play requires more than just a superficial knowledge of child development. The answer to the question is easy – one cannot recognise what is not known. Observing a set of developmental skills on their own often does not work if the observer is unable to evaluate, extend or facilitate further learning. A checklist approach can point the way, but a checklist cannot do the thinking, increase understanding, or help us to help children thrive. Early Years educators must be able to recognise this for themselves and not just at a superficial level.

Many Early Years educators do not realise how important play is and why they must observe it. Instead, adults are often seen hovering over children, waiting to pour skills into empty vessels rather than building on what is already known. Early Years educators need to understand how to use their knowledge of how children learn, with observations to guide them on when to intervene and when to withdraw and let children play. Moylett (2018:9) notes:

> Children's experiences in the early years lay the foundation for how they learn, with far-reaching effects through their school years and beyond. Rather than observation and reflection on how children learn being an afterthought in early years observation, assessment and planning practice, we need first and foremost to celebrate and support children as learners through recognising the importance of play, active learning and creative and critical thinking.

In general, Early Years educators tend to observe when there is an adult-led activity. However, when the children are in areas of continuous provision, and their play is more child-led, adults tend not to observe – either because they are always taking focus groups, so there is nobody available to observe the learning from those child-initiated moments, or this kind of play is seen as essentially unimportant, trivial and lacking in serious purpose. On the contrary, there is always a reason, purpose and goal. Early Years educators need to understand that children are not wasting their time when they play – they are engaged in all kinds of learning. The role of the observer is to identify what information children are gathering when they play.

One of the defining characteristics of an effective observer is the ability to know when to step in and when to stand back and observe the process of struggle, exploration, manipulation, practice and repetition. This requires a deep knowledge of child development, thinking about the reason, purpose or goal of the child's play, and trying to find an answer. Accordingly, our understandings of play are the golden thread that weaves together ideologies, instructional practices, assessment techniques and curriculum guidance. Play gives voice and a sense of well-being to children in a non-threatening way. Without play, the intellectual growth of infants and young children will be stunted and learning will be rendered meaningless. To draw a comparison with an orchestra, play is the harmony and the different instruments and voices are an ensemble of children's different first-hand experiences, cultural practices and traditions. These experiences are not brought together in a haphazard way, but harmoniously constitute play. Play is the backbone of learning – it can be quiet, noisy, fast, slow, energised or solitary, chiming or beautifully discordant. Early Years educators need to learn how to improvise with infants and young children by tuning in reciprocally and collaboratively. In essence, play is at the heart of learning because it foregrounds children as active participants.

Early Years educators who work with infants and young children also need to be aware of what ideas and beliefs they hold about how children develop and learn. Any assumptions they hold about children have a direct influence on how they teach them, according to Bruce (1987). The universal set of principles below, based on and influenced by the principles outlined by Bruce, represents the knowledge, skills and understanding required to make observations of infants and young children.

1. Knowledge of child development is essential. Children go through stages of development and need adults who understand these stages in order to know what to expect from them.
2. Understanding that infants and young children learn while they play. They learn best when they are busy doing things that they are really interested in and want to do.
3. Knowing how children make their internal and external thinking visible through schemas.

4. Understanding how play coordinates children's learning.
5. Early Years educators should be concerned with all areas of development and learning. These include physical, emotional, social, linguistic and cognitive development. These fit closely together, overlapping and influencing each other. We cannot separate physical development from social or cognitive development. Being able to work across the whole curriculum includes knowledge of how to develop children's skills and introduce new experiences.
6. Ability to continually observe children and provide them with the right conditions for development and learning.
7. Learning when to intervene and when to withdraw – let children solve their own problems.
8. Understand that children are individual and will learn and develop at their own pace. Children of the same age might not always be at the same stage of development. These differences, when observed, tell us something about how each child needs support and help.
9. Development and learning are important at all times and Early Childhood education must have the right conditions for children to thrive. That includes having well-trained and knowledgeable staff. It should not be about preparation for school but an important part of life. Each stage of the child's development should be sustained by adults responding to and supporting that stage.
10. Early Years educators have a pedagogical responsibility to share knowledge of how children develop and learn with their parents. Children learn at home, school and from other people. They are members of a family, community and culture and should not be seen in isolation but as an interaction within and between the environment in which the child lives.

Embedding these principles into professional practice takes time. But the more that Early Years educators know about how young children play, develop and learn, the more they will be able to use this knowledge to help them navigate their way around any curriculum documentation, and the stronger their pedagogical practice will become. In developing professional knowledge and observational skills, Early Years educators will be more informed and confident, able to help children to move beyond what they have done to learn new things, and to do some things in different ways. Above all we need to find ways to support the Early Years educators' pedagogical learning. This is perhaps why Work Group Supervision is so important (Manning-Morton, 2006; Elfer & Dearnley, 2007). Since Early Years educators have a wide range of knowledge and observational experience, those who have some knowledge of observation, child development and learning can help the others in the group.

Conclusion

Overall it may be said that it is essential for Early Years educators working with infants and young children to have a sound understanding of how they develop and learn. Early Years educators must also learn to thoroughly observe. As Elfer (2005:127) suggests, our reactions to our observations are all part of our subjective responses. Therefore, we need to consider how much time we give to Early Years educators to observe children's developing learning; what we are ready to see and/or consider and what they are ready to see, hear and take notice of.

In the next chapter we consider the connections between professional knowledge and observing significant learning.

Bibliography

Anning, A. & Edwards, A. (1999) *Promoting Children's Learning from Birth to Five: Developing the New Early Years Professional*. Buckingham: Open University Press.

Athey, C. (2009) *Extending Thoughts in Young Children: A Parent-Teacher Partnership*. 2nd edn. London: Paul Chapman.

Bruce, T. (1987) *Early Childhood Education*. London. Sydney: Hodder and Stoughton.

Bruce, T. (1991) *Time to Play in Early Childhood Education*. London: Hodder and Stoughton.

Bruce, T. (1997) 'Adults and Children Developing Play Together'. *Early Childhood*. 5 (1) pp. 89–99.

Bruce, T. (2019) *Educating Young Children: A Lifetime Journey into A Froebelian Approach. The Selected Works of Tina Bruce*. pp. 303–317 and pp. 349–352. London: Routledge.

Bruce, T., Elfer, P., & Powell, S. (2018) *The Routledge International Handbook of Froebel and Early Childhood Practice. Re-articulating Research and Policy*, pp. 299–300. London: Routledge.

Bruce, T., Louis, S., & McCall, G. (2015) *Observing Young Children*. London: Sage Publication Ltd.

Callanan, M., Anderson, M., Haywood, S., Hudson, R., & Speight, S. (2017) *Study of Early Education and Development: Good Practice in Early Education*. Research report, Department for Education.

Chukovsky, K. (1963) *From Two to Five*. Berkeley, CA/Los Angeles, CA/London: University of California Press.

Dalli, C. (2014) *Quality for Babies and Toddlers in Early Years' Settings*. Occasional paper 4, Association for the Professional Development of Early Years Educators. TACTYC, London.

Drummond, M. J. (2012) *Assessing Children's Learning*. London: Routledge.

Elfer, P. (2005) 'Observation Matters'. In: Abbott, L. & Langston, A. (eds) *Birth to Three Matters: Supporting the Framework of Effective Practice*. pp. 116–129. Maidenhead: Open University Press.

Elfer, P. & Dearnley, K. (2007) 'Nurseries and Emotional Well-being: Evaluating an Emotionally Containing Model of Professional Development'. *Early Years*. 27 (3) pp. 267–278.

Goouch, K. & Powell, S. (2013) *The Baby Room: Principles, Policy and Practice*. Maidenhead: Open University Press.

Louis, S. (2012) *Schemas and the Characteristics of Effective Learning*. London: Early Education.

Manning-Morton, J. (2006) 'The Personal Is Professional: Professionalism and the Birth to Threes Practitioner'. *Contemporary Issues in Early Childhood*. 7 (1) pp. 42–52.

Medwell, J., Wray, D., Poulson, L., & Fox, R. (1998) *Effective Teachers of Literacy. Summary of Findings: A Research Project by the University of Exeter*. Sponsored by the Teachers Training Agency.

Melhuish, E. (2014) *The Impact of Early Childhood Education and Care on Improved Well-being*. London: British Academy.

Moss, P. (2006) 'Structures, Understanding and Discourse: Possibilities for Re-envisioning the Early Childhood Worker'. *Contemporary Issues in Early Childhood*. 7 (1) pp. 30–41.

Moss, P. & Dahlberg, G. (2008) 'Beyond Quality in Early Childhood Education and Care – Languages of Evaluation'. *New Zealand Journal of Teachers' Work*. 5 (1) pp. 3–12.

Moss, P. & Petrie, P. (2002) *From Children's Services to Children's Space*. London: Routledge, Falmer.

Moyles, J., Adams, S., & Musgrove, A. (2002) *Study of Pedagogical Effectiveness in Early Learning*. London: DfES.

Moylett, H. (2018) 'Helping Young Children Become Great Learners: Observing and Supporting Self-regulation'. *Early Education*. 84, pp. 7–9.

Nutbrown, C. (2013) *Shaking the Foundations of Quality: Why 'Childcare' Policy Must Not Lead to Poor-Quality Early Education and Care*. Sheffield UK: The School of Education. The University of Sheffield.

Nutbrown Review. (2012) *Foundations for Quality: The Independent Review of Early Education and Childcare Qualifications. Final Report*. London Department for Education.

Siraj-Blatchford, I., Sylva, K., Muttock, S., Gilden, R., & Bell, D. (2002) *Researching Effective Pedagogy in the Early Years*. (REPEY), DFES (Department for Education and Skills) research report 356. DFE, London.

Stephen, C. (2010) 'Pedagogy: The Silent Partner in Early Years Learning'. *Early Years*. 30 (3) p. 28.

Stewart, N. (2011) *How Children Learn: The Characteristics of Effective Early Learning*. London: Early Education.

Urban, M. (2010) "Rethinking Professionalism in Early Childhood: Untested Feasibilities and Critical Ecologies'. Editorial'. *Contemporary Issues in Early Childhood*. 11 (1) pp. 1–7.

3 What do we see when children play?

Is observation just part of the paperwork? How often do you monitor the content of observations? Do observations capture significant learning or are they superficial? Is the information factual and useful? How often do you check that observations are accurate records? These questions and more are intended to challenge leaders and managers about their own practice.

It can be confusing for some educators watching a young child exploring a particular concept and not understanding what might be going on. Often young children appear to be busy doing nothing but there is always a reason or goal. The more that managers know about the structure of play, the more they can prioritise how educators observe what is going on. Managers need to be able to recognise what kind of learning is taking place – it does not help educators if managers are uninformed about how children learn.

This chapter is intended to support managers to develop their team's personal and professional skills and knowledge by actively reflecting on their observational practice. It also enables them to provide targeted support for those Early Years educators who have inadequate knowledge of what happens in play. More importantly, it enables managers to support Early Years educators to articulate and locate themselves in their practice, something there is often little time to do. Given how important this is, it is necessary to consider what the Early Years educators are learning from observations in order to help them to support development and learning in children.

In this chapter, leaders and managers will gain insight into what kind of learning is going on for children. This will help them to develop their knowledge so that they can provide Work Group Supervision effectively. How does one know that Early Years educators and their managers are capable of performing observational tasks? The process of making observations is more than just technical – it also includes the ability to translate knowledge into practice, make decisions, and thoughtfully respond. It is a complex interplay of personal and professional knowledge, skills, attitudes and values and this also includes one's limitations. On the one hand, supervision must include work performance. On the other, it simultaneously focuses on observations and assessments – for example, children not making progress – which are specific to developing and improving the practice of Early Years educators. The focus should not just be on negative situations but should also embrace positive experiences so that this learning can be shared across the team.

The ability to effectively lead and manage a team of Early Years educators is vital for children's progress. However, this is something many managers are not confident with and may not yet have the skills and knowledge required. The role of a manager in supporting teams of Early Years educators is both demanding and challenging. The manager's knowledge base is important here – how strong or weak it is may potentially have a direct influence on their motivation as an individual and on their organisation. This chapter looks more closely at the complexity and connection involved in children's play.

It is essential that adults working with babies and young children recognise and identify symbolic play, as well as acquiring and understanding the opportunity for learning and knowing how to support and extend play appropriately. Liebschner (1992:53) says:

> Froebel lists three different types of play. He differentiates between symbolic play, consisting of representations of ordinary life: creative play, where the material used is the only limiting factor and imitative play, which 'freely recreates' what has been learned in school. He adds that play presupposes an active and purposeful life in and out of school. Such a life will produce rich play which in turn will enhance life.

Unpicking play

Play is the natural way for young children to learn and it is a vital part of the process. It brings together different aspects of learning into a network and harmonises them. It also helps children to understand and make sense of what they have learned from ideas, feelings and relationships.

Play can help children make connections and realise what they know and understand. It is not the only strategy that children use but it is an important one. Bruce (1997:8) reinforces this. She argues that features of play embed and coordinate learning from a network of experiences. These kinds of play – games with rules, competence, wallowing, metacognition and representations of how children make sense of those experiences – we will explore here. Importantly, the network for learning demonstrates how play helps to develop children's thinking and imagination. It is in these ways that children are able to learn new skills and think of new ideas. Besides, play allows children to deal with their fears and fantasies, putting them in control of their learning. As we will see, play has a number of elements and provides learning in many overlapping ways.

Similarly, Piaget and Inhelder (1969) say that infants and young children need to find out about the world around them through their actions and note that they learn best through experience with real things, constructing knowledge through play. This knowledge is combined with what they already know to create a new understanding. Zosh et al. (2017) provide further evidence that children learn in the first instance through first-hand experience. They suggest that self-initiated activities help children to develop a number of skills, such as language and communication, symbolic representation, mathematics, scientific concepts, technology and design, reading, writing and problem-solving skills. According to Zosh et al. (2017), adults have an essential role to play in supporting children to engage in how to make sense of the world around them. Piaget (Piaget & Inhelder, 1969) notes that it is through the process of active learning, discovery and solving problems in play that infants and young children develop the thinking skills to organise and analyse knowledge. Through pretend play, children learn to navigate the world in which they live, especially their social world, by copying and imitating in their play what they see other people doing. Most importantly, through pretend play children learn about symbols, which is important for later mathematics, reading and writing.

Think of all the things that you do with the children every day; in the context of such routines, children begin to make sense of their world. However, is there enough time allowed for children to develop the characteristics of effective learning? How Early Years educators create a welcoming and enabling learning environment with a flexible routine is important because this will give children time to become absorbed in practising newly-acquired skills. It is from standing back and continually watching children that adults learn about what they are curious and interested in. There are many different types of pretend play which children enter into – this will depend on the child's age and the experience he or she has had with pretend play. For Froebel (1826) in Lilley (1967:83): "Play is the highest expression of human development in childhood for it alone is the free expression of what is in the child's soul." Play therefore should not be left to chance – it is not trivial and there is always a reason, purpose and aim to it. Nearly 240 years after Friedrich Froebel's pioneering work on play, it is timely to stop and think about why understanding the structure of play is so important in the observational process. Here are some examples.

Exploration

Babies will engage in exploratory play of their bodies and practise those first discoveries, like finding their feet by chance and putting them in their mouth.

What do we see when children play?

Imitation

One example would be a child fascinated by household objects – they may imitate simple everyday experiences such as feeding a doll, reading a book, hoovering or sweeping, or putting a doll to bed.

Pretend Play 1

A child may feed a "baby" or pretend to drink from a cup and will use things that look real, such as a doll for a baby and a real cup. When we observe children around the world engaged in this type of play, they are connecting with their first-hand experiences by pretending to be mummy or daddy.

Pretend Play 2

Here children begin more complex play with objects used as symbols of real things. For example, they may use a block for bread or a telephone; buttons can become play food; bottle tops can become play money, or a round paper plate a steering wheel. This is an important aspect of development.

Fantasy F

Children may pretend to be mum or dad, builders, shopkeepers and shoppers, doctors and nurses etc. They play in much more detail, for example, the "mother" may feed her baby, prepare breakfast, iron clothes and then take the children to school. Here children have reached a much higher level of symbolic play.

Phantasy Ph

Phantasy Ph is about children pretending to be fairies, dinosaurs, superheroes or animal characters, such as dogs or cats. Children will play out their Phantasy scenarios to explore a range of different roles, ideas and feelings of power. Superhero play, for example, is more often than not vigorous. In this way children are learning how to control and move their bodies by climbing as a spider, jumping, running to the Bat Cave and chasing villains. The difference between Fantasy and Phantasy is that in Fantasy play it is possible for a child to one day become a fireman, doctor/nurse, shopkeeper, builder, train/bus/taxi driver, or barber/hairdresser if they choose – but with Phantasy play a child can never become a dinosaur.

Storying

Children's narrative representations support the development of disembedded thinking. Children create stories to represent their understanding of their first-hand experiences. They will use their stories to reflect and act upon their knowledge.

Games

Games help children learn about how rules are made, how to keep them and how to negotiate to change them. For example, my daughter used to play a game in the bath every night. She would hide objects with the flannel or bubbles and say: "This is magic, what do you think is under there?" (I always had to guess the wrong object). This hiding game was entirely controlled by Hannah. The rules she made during her play would fade when bath time was finished.

Games can also help children to be part of their culture and cultivate a sense of belonging, and they differ according to different cultures. For example, whilst in South Africa recently, I observed a group of girls playing a game with stones, similar to a game called Jacks that I used to play with my sisters as a child, involving picking up objects while a ball is in the air. However, as they were playing with stones, and not the superball used in Jacks, I did not understand their rules. A friend told me that my game sounded very like a game he played as a child in Scotland, with stones or cubes of wood and no ball. Chuck one stone in the air, pick one off the ground, catch the descending one. Games can be related to individual teams, performance, social standing, socialisation, mathematics (addition and subtraction) and interest in sport.

Competence

Competence is about children gaining both control and mastery. Children will need to explore, manipulate, practise newly-acquired skills and be able to repeat things again and again. They learn how things change, how they are alike and how they are different – they learn how to make a ball out of dough, roll it, flatten it and make it into a ball once more, and notice that the ball will roll and a square block will not. Children develop competence through time to play with toys and materials. According to Tina Bruce (1991:65), "play is about participants wallowing in ideas, feelings and relationships. It involves reflecting on and becoming aware of what we know, or 'metacognition'."

Wallowing in ideas

In this example, Leon pretends to be going to the shop to buy milk and bread. He says to Josh, "Pretend that we are shopkeepers and we can eat all the sweets."

This play demonstrates Leon's ability to think about future roles that he might take up when he is older. Enacting these future roles is an important aspect of development.

Wallowing in feelings

Sarah is deeply involved in putting her doll in a pram and taking it to nursery. She tells the doll (named Sarah) that she is going to work and she must not cry – Sarah reassures the doll that she will pick her up later. She says, "They will look after you while I am gone." In this example, Sarah is exploring her feelings about being taken to nursery and left there.

Wallowing in relationships

It is difficult to distract Joseph from his drawing – he spends the whole time focused on a picture of himself with daddy driving to nursery. Joseph also wallows in the same relationship theme in other activities. He will spend a considerable amount of time making cars and pasting different materials together for his daddy. Wallowing allows children to grapple with their important relationships in a way that makes sense to them, through activities that they like and have chosen themselves.

Metacognition

Wallowing links in with metacognition; it involves self-review, knowing what you know and disembedded thinking – the ability to think about things that are not embedded in context or experience. Donaldson (1978:78) states that "when children are asked to do something outside their limits of human sense, that is when something is unfamiliar or unrealistic, their thinking is disembedded and it fails to make sense."

Symbolic representation

Children communicate what is important to them and how they feel about things through symbolic representations – for example, by constructing models, clay sculptures and modelling of play dough. Children's symbolic representations need to be based on their own first-hand experiences and not those of other people. In many ways, children's representations are a way of keeping hold of an experience. Symbolic representation is a process that ends in a product through which children show their view and understanding of the world.

Drawings, painting and models

Daniel draws a picture which shows two suns. When the adult asks him to talk about his drawing, he tells her that the second sun is a reflection in the water. Children's symbolic representations will mirror their first-hand experiences – it's no good asking a child to draw a hamster if they have never seen one. Adults need to be mindful that children's symbolic representations may not resemble the real object; this will come later.

Block play: This is free-standing wooden block play

Sequence 1

During the first sequence, children may spend a long time watching, touching or holding onto blocks. Some children like to carry them around. Some will see how many blocks they can carry without dropping them. They are finding out what blocks feel like – that some blocks are light, and some are heavy. In this sequence, children might use blocks symbolically to represent things in their everyday life.

Sequence 2

In the second sequence, children begin to build simple vertical or horizontal buildings by putting blocks together in rows, or by stacking one block onto another. It is through this type of repetitive exploration that children learn about concepts such as size and shape. They also learn how to balance blocks on top of each other, as well as building them upwards. In this way children begin to develop problem-solving and thinking skills as they discover the properties of blocks and learn about weight, balance and gravity. It is important that children are exposed to blocks daily so that they can fully explore them in new and different ways.

Sequence 3

During the third sequence, children begin to arrange blocks with a space, using another block to connect them as a bridge. Some children combine three blocks in the same way to form a bridging pattern. This bridging can become more and more sophisticated, with some children becoming fascinated with slopes and curves as another way of connecting through bridging.

What do we see when children play?

Sequence 4

During the fourth sequence, children begin to construct linear or circular buildings. They can build complex structures that represent things in their everyday life.

Sequence 5

During the fifth and final sequence children may be observed planning with other children. Often this will involve constructing a whole scene, rather than an isolated section, and representing it in different ways – for example, a house on a street might well be seen in the child's drawings at around the same time as they construct one with blocks. Or the child might have a preferred medium, with drawings or clay work coming ahead of block play, or the reverse. Children name and occupy themselves with their buildings in their fantasy and imaginary play, often actively constructing stories or parts of stories. As children begin to think things through, they negotiate their play agenda of what and how they are going to build. They may also include other props in their play.

Observing block play learning

During the earlier sequences of this type of play, children are getting to know the blocks. Look out for what particularly fascinates them. Are they learning about weight, balance and gravity as they explore and lift blocks of different sizes? Are they discovering the properties of the blocks, such as how to balance them on top of each other, or what happens when you build upwards? Children will learn how to prevent their structures from falling down or that heavier blocks are easier to balance if they are held in the middle. Playing with blocks helps children to learn about space as they begin to move them around. They also learn associated vocabulary, beginning to use and understand positional words such as on top, next to, or underneath. Look out for when children begin to be symbolic and pretend that something represents something else. Is it a shop? A bridge? A river or pond? Some children begin to pretend in this way quite early on, while others are not so interested.

In the third sequence, children experiment with building enclosed spaces, bridges, slopes, roofs and patterns. They learn about the shapes of individual blocks, how they fit together in a certain space, and how to combine them into many different shapes in their enclosures. It is in this way that young children become familiar with shapes informally in their play, making things beautiful in the way they use patterns, introducing their everyday life experiences. The adult's role is crucial in discussing with them what they are doing, extending their knowledge about shapes, balancing, joining and connecting. This is also how mathematical knowledge, such as fractions and measurement, emerges in block play. For example, the child learns that four smaller blocks equal two rectangle blocks, or by stretching their arms they can show the height of their building.

In the fourth sequence we begin to see developments in fantasy play with blocks. Children construct whole scenarios, rather than isolated constructions, and they often enjoy doing this with other children, working collaboratively together (Gura, 1992). They will use blocks to build houses, garages and roads, farms and airports and make up a narrative to go with it.

During the fifth sequence, children's block play shows us what they are thinking, what interests them and what is important to them. We see them being able to plan or to work collaboratively with other children, negotiating their ideas and being helpful so that the scenario or story develops in a way that pleases the group. Adults who are careful observers of block play are increasingly able to help children to extend and develop what they are doing, as well as the learning related to it.

Construction: construction kits where things join, such as Lego and Dulpo are different to free-standing wooden block play

A group of boys aged 4 and 5 years are observed in the construction area building tunnels, ramps and bridges. The boys persevere at building the tunnel for their play to continue. At times they work together and at others they work alone. When they finish, they knock the whole thing down. These children are learning important things about design and balance and adults need to observe how children represent their experiences in their block and construction play.

Malleable materials e.g. using clay, play dough, mud pies

Helen, who has recently celebrated her third birthday, makes Robina a birthday cake. Robina alters the shape of the cake by rolling it out and offering Helen a poppadom. Helen is re-enacting a recent experience. Robina is learning about transforming things. She knows that dough alters its shape when rolled. Transforming is not a schema but comes about as a result of exploring schematic play (see chapter on schemas).

Conclusion

Thus, play for children is a natural and important part of growing up. However, symbolic play gives children an opportunity to make connections, take control, to make decisions and rules. When children pretend that they are going to work on the train or going to the doctors, their fantasy play is helping them to understand their first-hand experience and/or fears. Playing and interacting with the adult with whom the child is making key attachments, gives the child permission or ideas about what is possible. The play that children wallow in can be a great source of joy and engender a sense of peace and quiet of feeling secure and at one with oneself – shaping a sense of identity. Play is not just about making sense of the world, but it is also about making sense of ourselves and our emotional well-being. We need to consider how Early Years educators' knowledge and understanding of play influences children's explorations and investigations.

In the next chapter we discuss the importance of educators being able to recognise and respond to children developing schemas.

Bibliography

Bruce, T. (1991) *Time to Play in Early Childhood Education*. London: Hodder and Stoughton.

Bruce, T. (1997) '"Adults and Children Developing Play Together". European Early Childhood Education Research Journal'. *Early Childhood*. 5 (1) pp. 89–99.

Donaldson, M. (1978) *Children's Minds*. London: Collins/Fontana.

Dowling, M. (2013) *Young Children's Thinking*. London: Sage.

Gura, P. (1992) *Exploring Learning. Young Children and Blockplay*. London: Paul Chapman Publishing Ltd.

Liebschner, J. (1992) *A Child's Work: Freedom and Guidance in Froebel's Educational Theory and Practice*. Cambridge: The Lutterworth Press.

Lilly, I. M. (1967) *Friedrich Froebel. A Selection From His Writing*. Cambridge: Cambridge University Press.

Louis, S. (2012) *Schemas and the Characteristics of Effective Learning*. London: Early Education.

Moylett, H. (2014) *The Characteristics of Effective Early Learning: Helping Children to Become Learners for Life*. Maidenhead: Open University Press.

Nutbrown, C. (2011) *Threads of Thinking: Schemas and Young Children's Learning*. 4th edn. London: Sage.

Piaget, J. & Inhelder, B. (1969) *The Psychology of the Child*. London: Routledge & Kegan Paul.

Zosh, J. M., Hopkins, E. J., Jensen, H., Liu, C., Neale, D., Hirsh-Pasek, K., Solis, S. L., & Whitebread, D. (2017). *Learning through play: a review of the evidence (white paper)*. The LEGO Foundation, DK.

4 Schemas
The key to patterns of behaviour

One of the main challenges facing the Early Childhood workforce is how to explain what significant learning is taking place as babies and young children interact with people, objects, nature resources and materials in their setting. What often seems like chance exploration can be better explained by understanding repeated behaviours or "schemas". These are defined by Chris Athey (1990:5) as "patterns of behaviour and thinking in children that exist underneath the surface features of various contents, contexts and specific experiences". Recent neuroscience has revealed that children need to be able to repeat things around 360 times to develop and master a skill. This chapter will explore schemas as a learning mechanism and as a helpful observational tool that adults can use to develop children's thinking.

An important part of Work Group Supervision is being able to reflect on observations. The process is intended to help educators look more carefully at children and consider what ideas they might be exploring or what they may be interested in. So often observations reveal that some children are exploring particular schematic concepts. Educators need to understand that schemas play a crucial role in the wiring of infants and young children's brains. This is echoed by Shore (1997:17), who states that:

> In early years, children's brains form twice as many synapses as they will eventually need. If these synapses are used repeatedly in a child's day-to-day life, they are reinforced and become part of the brain's permanent circuity. If they are not used repeatedly, or often enough, they are eliminated.

Through their ongoing observations of children, adults will know that schematic behaviours are already evident. From birth, babies can be observed repeatedly grasping, lifting, sucking, mouthing, kicking, waving and banging. As they do this, they explore early schematic actions, which aid their earliest learning. These early schematic behaviours later become more complex, with children coordinating their actions (Nutbrown, 1999). Initially, a baby reflexively makes circular motions. However, when we see toddlers making deliberate circular arm and limb movements, they are displaying related behaviour, which has an underlying pattern running through it. These are developed and refined and will come to include rolling, spinning and turning. These physical and sensory movements coordinate with the positioning and orientation schema.

What is a schema?

A schema is a repeated action, often seen in the behaviours of babies and young children. They have a natural urge to do the same thing again and again, whether it is the grasping, sucking and mouthing of babies or the toddler throwing things, hiding things in bags, or emptying all the toys out of the toy box. This repetitive behaviour helps children to develop and deepen their understanding of concepts. Have you ever noticed that if a child does something schematically, they do it more than twice? For example, Vicky puts on a jacket from the role-play area and then starts to play I Spy with an empty Pringles container. She then puts on a waistcoat, on top of the jacket. Next, she finds a kitchen roll tube, puts this inside the Pringles container and again plays I Spy. Whatever she does with the materials and resources, she also does to herself. Schemas link directly to how the young brain develops and grows. As children repeat actions, they make important connections in their brains, which help them to modify their actions or make changes. This is a vitally important element in young children's development and learning. Children need opportunities to practise repeatedly what they know and can do, so that what is known becomes better known.

Observing schemas

Adults need to observe the developing learning of each child and find out what motivates and interests them. Observations need to be a continuous, formative assessment, so that adults get to know the child's relationships, learning, interests and needs. The adults need to look at all the observations every few weeks, discuss them with colleagues and parents, and plan what to do next based on this summative assessment.

It is vital for adults to understand that schemas are not new; they are biological and what children do as a fundamental aspect of their development. Schemas are often characterised as a type of play that is essentially unimportant, trivial and lacking in any serious goal. On the contrary, repeated actions and behaviours help children to become more familiar with what they know and can do. It is in this way that children make their thinking visible. When adults working with babies and young children discover the meaning behind repeated schematic behaviour in a range of contexts and situations, they will find understanding in seeing that some of what the children do can be explained and accepted. For example, in patterns of action and behaviour related to understanding area and estimating size, volume and capacity, toddlers are often observed putting their thumb or finger(s) in and out of their mouths, or filling and emptying bags and containers of all kinds. They climb into large and small boxes, baskets, suitcases, sit under an apparatus, occupy small spaces or tunnels, build enclosures with bricks, and put borders around their paintings. Although these activities may seem unrelated, children are in fact working hard on a schematic underlying pattern of behaviour, which is not random, but deliberate and systematic.

Adults may not know that there are times when children's play is completely schematic. Children use schemas to understand important abstract mathematical and scientific concepts. When these early schematic behaviours are supported, extended and deepened by adults, they become firm foundations on which to build the children's future learning. Atherton and Nutbrown (2013) talk about "tuning in conceptually to children's exploration" and even trying to think about the concepts that children might be exploring with. Early Years educators need to understand that schemas can be seen as mentally organised categories into which a child's knowledge and experiences fit. Informed observations are a fundamental characteristic of good teaching. The ability to observe schematic play and respond appropriately to children, being informed by ones knowledge of developing learning.

- Have you recognised any schematic patterns of behaviour?
- What do you think the child is exploring?
- How would you describe the learning taking place?
- How could you support and enrich the child's experiences?
- What changes would you make to the learning environment to support the child's schemas?
- How can you deepen the child's learning?
- Are there children in your setting who are displaying irritating and challenging behaviour that is schematic? If yes, in what ways can you redirect their play?

Adults helping children to learn

By understanding schemas, adults can support and encourage children to play and learn in a way that links to the child's schematic interests. Schemas are often seen when babies and young children are given opportunities to lead their own play.

Adults need to provide children with a stimulating learning environment so that they can explore and practise newly-acquired skills and repeat child-initiated play which sets up a foundation for lifelong learning.

Schemas help us to organise and process our thoughts and feelings. They help us to think. As we get older our schemas do not go away, they just get more sophisticated. Knowledge of schemas can help adults to give detailed descriptions of the ways in which the child is approaching learning. Adults can use this knowledge to help them to understand the child's behaviour, motivation and learning as it develops.

Schemas can be observed as operating in four different ways. These include:

Sensory and movement development

A child may explore flour, as an example, through their actions and senses, by moving it from place to place, throwing it, tasting it, studying it and touching it. What is important here is that these sensory experiences stimulate the child's brain.

Symbolic representation: Pretend Play 1

This is when children pretend to be doing things, such as having a drink, or feeding teddy. For example, one child is observed with a bowl under her jumper. The adult asks her if she is pregnant and she says: "No it's a bowl." Although what she is doing is enacted in a symbolic way, she does not yet understand the symbolism that she is using. In this play, children require resources that are similar to the real object, for example, a doll representing a baby, or a plate for a wheel. It is important to note that if children do not have access to resources such as dolls then the literal experience of seeing babies being cared for becomes important.

Pretend Play 2

This is when children use one thing to stand in for another. A child might mix sand and stones in a bowl to pretend (represent) that they are cooking food or pretend that the books scattered on the floor are a river. Here children are able to apply their knowledge and experiences to their play.

Symbolic representation helps develop the whole child, as well as offer a fun aspect of childhood while boosting social skills and allowing children to learn new skills or knowledge through kinesthetic movement. It also offers an opportunity to practise speech and increase exposure to and understanding of varying emotions. There is also the mature play seen when children say a tree with hollows and knots on the trunk is described as a fairy palace. Children have brought together several literal, direct experiences – grand buildings, imaginary people called fairies and where they live – but still making use of real experience to bring about imaginative alternative worlds.

Cause and effect

This is how children demonstrate through actions that they understand cause and effect relationships. For example, when playing a child might use a tea towel or oven gloves to take the cake out of the oven.

Thought

Children begin to reflect upon and become more aware of their own knowledge, such as a child being able to verbally tell you about an experience without the aid of any of the materials or resources they have used. In this example, Bruce, Louis and Bloch (2019:30) observe the following conversation between a child and a practitioner:

> The child noted the effects of stuffing lots of toilet tissues into the plughole. The child said, 'I put tissue in the plughole and the paper got wet'. The practitioner later asked what happens when you completely block the sink and the child said, 'the water cannot get out'.

Athey (1990) suggests that when children reach the "thought level", the earlier motor and representational stages with all the content of past experiences are "brought forward" to provide the "form" and "stuff" of thinking, so that they are better able to explain things.

Each of these ways is equally important. It is vital that adults provide children with access to continuous resources and materials, both indoors and outdoors, so that they can absorb information through their senses. Adults can support children's pretend play by providing materials from their everyday experience such as meal time, bed time, going shopping etc. This will help children to become more familiar with and make sense of their experiences.

Identifying schemas

Schemas are a way of describing common behaviour patterns in seemingly unrelated activities. They help us to describe in more detail the way in which a child is approaching a self-initiated activity and following it through. This helps adults to better understand children's play and to provide appropriately for individual children. A knowledge and understanding of schemas give adults a language for describing the complexities and connections within children's play. Some examples of common biological schemas are:

- Trajectory
- Rotation
- Enclosing
- Containing
- Enveloping
- Transporting
- Positioning
- Orientation
- Connection and disconnection
- Core and radial

The Trajectory schema

A child might be interested in moving or exploring straight lines and will represent lines with toys. Children might also put wooden blocks next to each other; pour water into funnels and water wheels; try to catch water coming out of a watering can. They are learning about height, speed, distance and how things move.

Observation of Thomas, aged 2 years and 1 month

Thomas likes to climb and jump on and off furniture, walk along the edge of lawns, kick balls, and throw objects. He is often observed outside, repeatedly going up and down the climbing frame. He also likes to play with a pulley, pulling an empty bucket up and down.

Observation of Jay, aged 2 years and 11 months

Jay has discovered that a ball rolls faster down guttering than a truck and even faster if he balances the gutter on the bench. He says: "More quick."

Adults will need to think about how they can support Thomas with opportunities to climb into, onto, over and under things, to roll, crawl, jump and run throughout the day, indoors as well as outdoors. Thomas's play is physical as he is developing strength. He is also learning about height and weight through moving up and down. Thomas is practising his newly-acquired skills by pulling the bucket higher and then lowering it.

He is exploring with cause and effect. Jay is in the process of understanding that if you increase the steepness of the guttering, the ball rolls much faster. He is also beginning to organise, group and compare things. He expresses this understanding through his language. Adults can help Jay to play by supporting his explorations in discovering the object's features and their relationship. This is the beginning of scientific thinking.

The Rotation schema

A child might be interested in how they can make things move and turn (cause and effect). Mixing ingredients together; rolling balls up and down hill; spinning around in circles to music; playing with cars or trains and watching carefully how the wheels move backwards and forwards. Through their exploration children develop an understanding of how they and objects turn.

Observation of Samantha, aged 2 years and 4 months

Samantha is interested in things that turn, spin and twist. She is often observed pushing an empty buggy round and round or running and spinning around herself. At home, her mum reports that she pushes her empty buggy around the kitchen table. She also often makes frequent requests to be swung around by adults. For several weeks she is also observed to be painting circles and spiral patterns that fill many of her pictures.

Samantha is exploring the concept of rotation. Through the physical use of her body she is also developing an understanding about how circular movements behave and is able to demonstrate this symbolically and imaginatively in her paintings, and in other play choices.

The Enclosing schema

The enclosure schema has no fixed bottom joined to the sides. The earliest enveloping schemas are babies putting their thumbs into their mouths. A child might construct an enclosure in which they put animals in a field. It is related to filling and emptying. Filling and emptying become related to estimating size, shape, measurement and volume of spaces.

Observation of Eddie, aged 2 years and 9 months

Eddie likes to build enclosures with blocks and containers. He describes his enclosures as ponds for the ducks. Eddie likes to build cages with gates and is often seen building fields to enclose different groups of farm animals. Eddie is developing an understanding about sorting and classifying groups of items.

Observation of Paul, aged 3 years and 6 months

Sometimes Paul fills the enclosure and sometimes he leaves it empty. For example, Paul made a bears' cave out of clay; he said it was empty because the bear was out hunting.

Paul is developing an understanding about more, less, and the difference in quantity – full and empty.

The Containing schema

The containment schema has a bottom joined to the sides. Children interested in containing might have an urge to put resources inside of a bucket, basket, bag, containers without a lid, and pots. The containing schema is often linked to the enveloping schema as some children may like to climb into boxes and baskets, and may also like filling up buckets with sand or water.

Observation of Milo, aged 2 years and 11 months

Milo repeatedly fills each compartment of a cupcake tray full of sand and spends time smoothing the top so that it is level. He tells the adult that he has made cakes. Later he pours sand from two different-sized containers into another, filling it to the top.

While transporting sand from one container to another, Milo is deeply immersed in exploring the concepts of accumulation and quantity.

The Enveloping schema

The enveloping schema is often observed in parallel with the enclosure and containing schema. The envelopment schema surrounds. Children might sit in a box with a lid over it. Adults may observe children wrapping things up or putting them in boxes with covers or lids. They may also wrap themselves up in a blanket or hide in boxes. Children sometimes do a drawing, then completely cover it with paint. Adults can assume that the children believe they have made a mistake or ruined their artwork. On the contrary, the children might have drawn a picture of them being under the duvet with mummy, put the cover over the bird cage that they have just drawn, closed the curtains, or drawn a picture of night-time. They are exploring the idea of completely covering objects, spaces and themselves. This links to the Piaget (1963) concept of object permanence, that things exist even though they may be out of sight.

Schemas: The key to patterns of behaviour

Children may also have an interest in dressing up and wearing masks – covering completely is envelopment and partial envelopment would be the mask covering the face. When children wear superhero outfits in doing so – they envelop parts of their body. Some children like to wear their selected outfit to pre-school or nursery. This can help children to feel more comfortable about transitions.

Observation of Sarah, aged 2 years and 3 months

Sarah likes to post items into enveloping spaces. She also likes to fit herself into an enveloping space (such as a box with a lid so that it surrounds her).

Sarah is developing an understanding of envelopment – box with lid over her.

Observation of India, aged 2 years and 7 months

India likes to dress up, fill containers, put things in bags, hide behind the curtains or beneath blankets, cover dolls with towels, wrap presents and parcels, and hide things in unusual places. Outdoors, she is observed crawling on the grass, with a piece of fabric over her body. When the adult asks her what she is doing, she replies: "I'm being a snail."

India is developing an understanding that things can still exist even when out of sight, known as object permanence (Piaget, 1963). She is motivated by things that disappear and spends much of her time concealing or covering things up, so that they are out of sight. As she repeats this type of play, she is developing the basics of knowledge about space, volume and capacity.

Observation of Hannah, aged 2

Hannah covers her hands and arms with paint.

Hannah is developing an understanding that paint will cover her hands and arms and that water will wash it off.

Observation of Alice, aged 2 years and 3 months

Alice likes to dress up and wrap dolls and other objects. She is regularly observed making nappies out of tissue to put on the dolls, dressing them up and wrapping them in a blanket ready for bed.

Alice is developing an understanding that she can use one object to stand in for another. Adults can help children to develop their play by ensuring that they provide resources for them to cover themselves or objects up. These could be small containers to put things into, or envelopes to put things inside something else. Adults can also provide big boxes, bags or tents that children can get into.

The Transporting schema

It can be very confusing to observe a toddler repeatedly putting all their bricks in a truck one at a time. Why do children enjoy doing this? They often seem to be engaged in doing nothing, but things are not always what they seem. Through moving objects, or a collection of objects, from one place to another, children learn about progressive changes in quantity – adding, taking away and sharing.

Observation of Angel, aged 2 years and 2 months

Angel likes to carry toys in bags, moving them from one place to another. She also enjoys pushing buggies with a teddy in them. She is frequently seen filling, pushing, pulling and dumping objects around the nursery.

Angel is in the process of developing an understanding about progressive changes in quantity by adding and taking away. In this way, children make judgements about quantity and movement by choosing to add or take away objects. This exploratory play helps to develop the children's ability to judge differences in amounts and is the first step to developing the skill of counting.

The Positioning schema

Here children are learning about order, sequencing, classification, shape, symmetry and one-to-one correspondence.

Observation of Elliot, aged 2 years and 9 months

Elliot spontaneously sorts a set of pots, matches each with a lid, then organises them on the shelf by size. Elliot likes to arrange lines; he lines up cars and trucks in size order. He also insists that they must face in the same direction. Elliot is observed painting two pictures. In the first, he covers the paper with random dabs. He says that the dabs are "lots, hundreds of people". In his second picture, he systematically places dabs in the centre of the paper and says that they are "animals in a field".

Elliot is developing an understanding about numbers; he is learning that dabs may be used to represent numbers that he understands. He will need adults to support him who can recognise and appreciate his symbolic mathematical representation of number and quantity.

The Orientation schema

The typical 2-year-old will need resources and materials to pull, push, fill, dump, ride on, slide down, jump on and crawl through. They also need spaces where they can run. The boys in the previous scenarios are learning to handle themselves physically. As they do so, they are finding out about their limits. They learn about balance, height, weight and width and are discovering how things look from different angles. Play helps them to make decisions for themselves.

Observation of Oscar, aged 2 years and 3 months

Oscar likes turning objects and himself around and upside down. He sometimes spins around.

Observation of Jade, aged 2

Jade likes to go through tunnels and come out of the other end.

Observation of Steven, aged 2

Steven likes climbing; he likes being at the top of the slide.
The children are finding out how things look from different angles. They learn about balance, height, weight and width.

Connecting and disconnecting schema

Children might be interested in building towers then knocking them down; play with construction toys, joining pieces together; join small pieces of play dough together to make a larger piece; make musical instruments from boxes and tubes; or complete jigsaw puzzles.

Observation of Joe, aged 3 years and 3 months

Joe joins five magnetic train carriages together and pulls them along the track, chanting "choo choo".
Joe is finding out about how to fasten things together using different materials. However, when engaged in disconnecting, children are reversing the connections made.

Schemas: The key to patterns of behaviour

Observation of Emma and Arthur, both aged 3

The twins spend much of the morning hammering nails into a piece of packing cardboard. Once it is completely covered with three long lines of nails, Arthur takes each nail out, one at a time, using a lever.

This shows that Arthur has understanding of connections and reversibility.

Observation of Peter, aged 4 years and 1 month

Peter is interested in disconnecting things. He likes knocking down towers and taking train tracks apart. Peter is also observed taking apart several hair bands then trying unsuccessfully to put them back together. Next he is seen taking an orange juice carton apart. He continues his exploration by repeating the actions of taking off the lid and releasing air by flattening out the carton. This shows that Peter has an understanding of reversible and irreversible.

Observation of Sima, aged 4

Sima empties the entire cupboard full of small boxes of books into a large pile in the middle of the room. When the cupboard is empty he looks really pleased with himself. Later, Sima takes all the shoes out of the bottom of the wardrobe in order to create a reading place. Sima shows that he has an understanding of, and an interest in, disconnecting.

Schema clusters

It is vital adults understand that all children have schemas. However, some children have one very clear schema; other children may have a number of schemas called clusters. Bruce (1997) provides a useful definition: "Schemas are patterns of linked behaviours, which the child can generalise and use in a whole variety of different situations. It is best to think of schemas as being a cluster of pieces which fit together."

The core and radial schema

Here children are learning how to combine enclosed shapes and lines in their drawings. Drawing circles and lines leads to representations and symbolic drawings.

Schemas: The key to patterns of behaviour

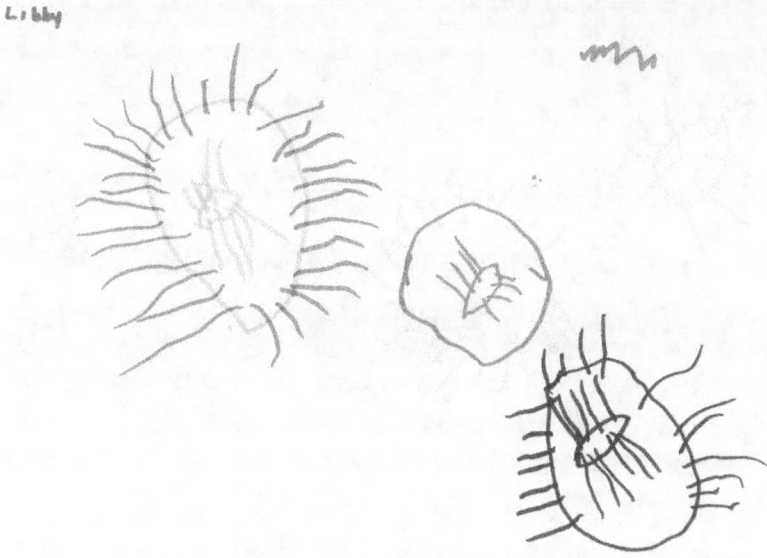

Figure 4.1 Enclosed spiders and some radials

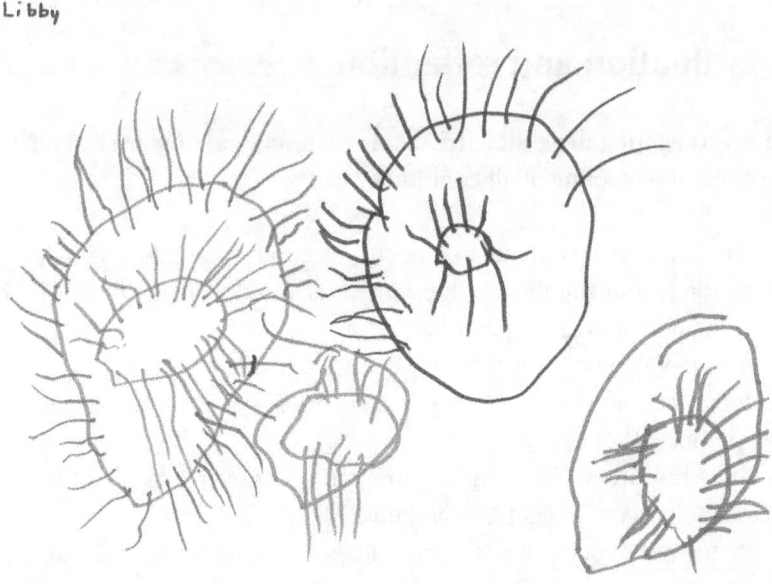

Figure 4.2 Spiders with centre marks. These radial marks are forerunners of the core and radial schema

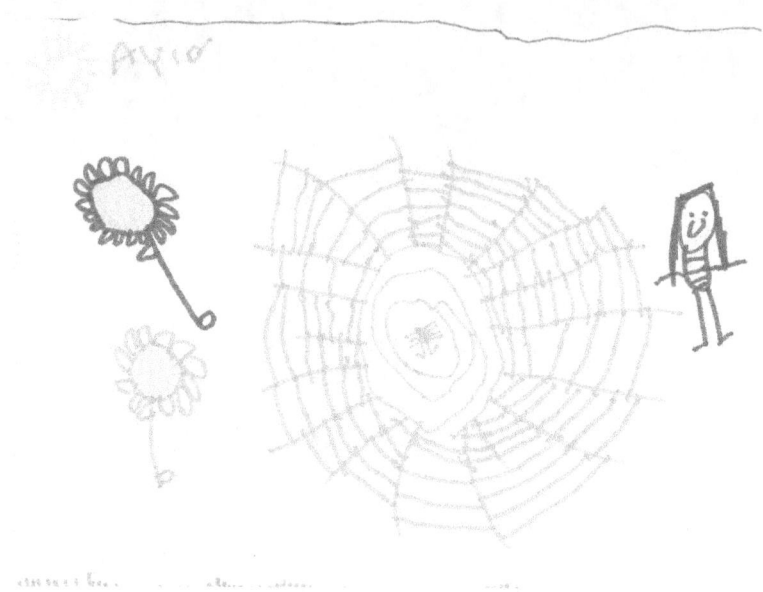

Figure 4.3 Flowers with looped petals. Radial figures, limbs arms and legs. Core and radial designed spiders' web

Evaluation and reflection

What are you offering the child? The social environment, the physical environment and the cultural environment all contribute.

- Are children making choices and decisions about what they play with?
- Are children concentrating on their interests and deeply involved? Are children practising and applying what they already know?
- Are they developing ideas that they can try out?
- Are there flexible spaces indoors and outdoors that children can use for their own purposes?
- Are there resources that children can jump on or over, kick a ball through, balance on, climb on and get into and under?
- Are there continuously available resources and natural materials for children to handle and transport freely?
- Are adults involved, interested and observing schematic play? Do observations inform action and planning?
- Are all adults knowledgeable and confident about the developing concept behind particular schemas?

Conclusion

In general, schematic play tends to be characterised as the type of play, which is essentially unimportant, trivial and lacking in any serious goal. It is often described as the kind of play that infants and young children sometimes engage with because they are naughty or perhaps bored. On the contrary, there is always a reason, purpose and goal why a child might, for example, spend a considerable amount of time going back and forth to bring us one block at a time. Early Years educators need to recognise that the child is not wasting their time but developing a deep understanding about their back and forth movements.

In this next chapter we have discussed the importance of educators being able to recognise and notice that schematic behaviours are meaningful. The next chapter turns our attention to Work Group Supervision.

Bibliography

Arnold, C. (2009) 'Understanding Together and Apart: A Case Study of Edward's Exploration at Nursery'. *Early Years.* 29 (2) pp. 119–130.

Arnold, C. and the Pen Green Team (2010) *Understanding Schemas and Emotions in Early Childhood.* London: Sage Publishing.

Atherton, F. & Nutbrown, C. (2013) *Understanding Schemas and Young Children: From Birth to Three.* London: Sage Publishing.

Athey, C. (1990) *Extending Thoughts in Young Children.* London: Paul Chapman.

Bruce, T. (1991) *Time to Play in Early Childhood Education.* London: Hodder and Stoughton.

Bruce, T. (1997) 'Adults and Children Developing Play Together'. *Early Childhood.* 5 (1) pp. 89–99.

Bruce, T. (2001) *Learning through Play: Babies, Toddlers and the Foundation Years.* London: Hodder and Stoughton.

Bruce, T., Louis, S., & Bloch, C. (2019) 'All about Schematic Learning'. *Nursery World.* 4–17 February 2019, pp. 25–30.

Bruce, T., Louis, S., & McCall, G. (2015) *Observing Young Children.* London: Sage Publications Ltd.

Louis, S. (2012) *Schemas and the Characteristics of Effective Learning.* London: Early Education.

Louis, S., Beswick, C., Magraw, L., & Hayes, L. (2008) *Again! Again! Understanding Schemas in Young Children.* Lutterworth: Featherstone Education.

Louis, S., Beswick, C., Magraw, L., & Hayes, L. (2012) *Understanding Schemas in Young Children. Again! Again!* London: Bloomsbury.

Nutbrown, C. (1999) *Threads of Thinking*. London: Paul Chapman.
Piaget, J. (1963) *The Psychology of Intelligence*. Totowa, NJ: Littlefield Adams.
Shore, R. (1997) *Rethinking the Brain*. New York: Families & Work Institute.

5 What is supervision?

Typically, subjective by nature, educators' observations are usually linked to their personal and professional understanding and beliefs about children's development and learning. Work Group Supervision focuses on unpicking educators' observations and their understanding of them. Focusing on observations in this way, by making the private public, can be unnerving for any educator, but it can also serve as an important tool for professional development – supporting them to examine their observational practice, solve common problems and apply new learning, and provide feedback. The main aim is to support educators to broaden their knowledge of child development and how children learn. Facilitating discussions and feedback relating to the observation – and how this information has been interpreted, understood and used by the observer, is a good way of reflecting on practice.

Observations tend to be most effective when the observer has a sound knowledge of child development, knows how to implement the relevant curriculum, understands the structure of play and can work together with other team members to reflect on and analyse children's behaviour. Observation is least effective when educators spend long periods waiting and watching for children to produce a set of skills which can be ticked off on a checklist, without understanding, analysis or dialogue with others. This is where Work Group Supervision can bring the greatest benefits, used as a means of sharing knowledge and understanding about how children develop and learn. For the educator struggling with observations, Work Group Supervision led by an external facilitator or the setting manager can provide invaluable support in improving their knowledge and observational skills. It is vital that group members draw up a rota for themselves to decide who will present and what child is to be discussed.

There are several different definitions of supervision but many similarities between them. Some place more significance on its organisational purpose while others concentrate on the individual. Hawkins and Shohet (2012) recognise the organisation as part of the "wider systemic context" and emphasise the collective professional responsibilities of the supervisor and those being supervised. They define supervision as a joint endeavour in which a practitioner, with the help of a supervisor, attends to their clients, themselves – as part of their client-practitioner relationships – and the wider systemic context. Doing so improves the quality of their work, transforms their client relationships, and continuously develops themselves, their practice and the wider profession.

What is Work Group Supervision?

Work Group Supervision is a continual process of rigorous professional learning in which Early Years educators are helped to develop their practice (Louis, 2017). During the session, Early Years educators are encouraged to reflect on and discuss their day-to-day observational practice while being offered an opportunity to enhance and develop their awareness of how children learn – the main purpose being to improve their observational practice by focusing on how they tune into children. These primary processes of discussion and reflection support Early Years educators to recall a sequence of observations and interpret them in order to gain a better and deeper understanding for further professional development. Reflection and discussion are fundamental to professional and personal development in the Early Childhood sector. Early Years educators' knowledge is rooted in their personal and professional experience – reflection on this is essential to professional practice. Work Group Supervision enables Early Years educators to discuss children's development and learning, interests and needs and relationships in a safe, supportive environment.

By contributing to the session, Early Years educators can receive support, feedback and guidance from colleagues to increase their understanding about how children develop and learn. In this regard, the Work Group Supervision is intended to serve as continuing professional training and development. Openly discussing specific observational issues is a good opportunity to establish consistent approaches toward child observations throughout the setting, while enhancing and deepening development and learning for individual children. Through sharing their understanding and knowledge about the children they work with, Early Years educators come to realise that they are not alone in their struggles, fears, feelings and perceptions, thus providing each other with reassurance and peer support.

Work Group Supervision fits well with functions of group supervision. These are fourfold; first, to provide a regular time and space for the Early Years educators to reflect upon the content and processes of their observational work; second, as part of a managerial administrative function; third, an educative function – building strengths, skills and knowledge, and receiving feedback from other perspectives about one's observational work, which promotes corroboration and support between colleagues, Bruce (1987) points out that the Froebelian mantra of observe, support and extend is a key part of the educative function; and fourth, motivational function – encouraging the team and individuals to get things done with the overall aim of growth and improvement.

Why supervision matters

An example of how Work Group Supervision can help Early Years educators is in the thorny question of gunplay (Holland, 2003). Universally, children take things such as sticks or blocks and use them as guns. Should Early Years educators support this play? In examining this, it may help to ask more questions before coming up with an answer. This is one of the reasons why Work Group Supervision is extremely important. It can help Early Years educators question the reasons behind the play, as opposed to making attempts at stopping it because they do not like guns and associated violence. Questions such as "Where did the children get their ideas?" or "Is the children's play a response to something that they have seen or experienced?" need to be asked. The issues of gunplay are complex and Early Years educators will need to understand that this kind of play may be the children's way of expressing their feelings or experiences.

Without knowledge of what happens in such play, Early Years educators may not encourage it, nor encourage the children to talk about their experiences and fears. This cannot be good for children's development or emotional well-being. The implications for the children's social and emotional development is that they may not be allowed to safely express and deal with their feelings, and may lack the ability to take the initiative or choose what they want to do. This will have a significant impact on their confidence and their attitude towards learning. Having a space to help Early Years educators develop their self-understanding of play, and the reasons behind the children's play and behaviour, is therefore very important. Work Group Supervision can provide them with an opportunity to express how they feel and talk to others about gunplay and other kinds of play, as a means to develop their understanding about how children learn.

There is very little reported research into group supervision with nursery staff. The closest comparable study is that of Jackson (2008) on the development of work group discussions in secondary schools. Research has tended to focus on individual support of teachers instead. An exception is the work of Hopkins (1988), a therapist working at the Tavistock Clinic in London, who believes that some nursery practices are harmful to children. Hopkins' (1988) research shows that providing Early Years educators with a secure group space to explore their thoughts and feelings about specific practice allows them to develop understanding. Two key characteristics of Hopkins' approach are that no teaching of any kind takes place and opportunities to talk about practice are encouraged. She argues that this allows the participants' own fears and anxieties to emerge and be explored. Meanwhile, Manning-Morton's

(2006:50) model of Continuing Professional Development (CPD) focuses on relationship-based learning. Manning-Morton encourages personal reflection on practice and theoretical thinking, which enables Early Years educators to develop both their practice and their professional identities. One of the key features of Manning-Morton's approach is the focus on personal and professional reflection.

Elfer and Dearnley (2007) promote an approach to CPD that is both didactic and interactive. Working with a group of 12 nursery heads, they explored the emotional challenges of their work and how the key person approach translated in practice. The heads were also encouraged to reflect on their feelings, enabling them to be more considerate about themselves and how they assisted their staff to support children's emotional needs. Two key features of this model are that the heads are encouraged to learn from experience and are provided with a reflective space.

While these studies clarify that engagement with emotional aspects of the role is important, they also indicate that Early Years educators start to notice children who were previously under the radar (Elfer & Dearnley, 2007) and this has the potential to change how children are observed. These studies also highlight a gap for an approach to support Early Years educators to develop professional learning. Finally, the findings also suggest that providing space for Early Years educators to reflect on observation, assessment and planning skills in small group supervision sessions may help to develop their understanding and practice and improve outcomes for children.

Conclusion

Finally, it may be concluded that supervision matters to all of those that work with and care for infants and young children; because the process is designed to support, motivate and enhance professional practice for individuals and teams of Early Years educators. As a result, this improves their knowledge base, quality of observation, interaction, talk and play. Supervision is therefore a significant part of how leaders and managers provide support and training for individual professional development. We need to think about the opportunities that we provide for Early Years educators to have supervision with a supervisor that can support them both educationally and emotionally.

The next chapter looks at combining Work Group Supervision and observation.

Bibliography

Bruce, T. (1987) *Early Childhood Education*. London: Hodder & Stoughton.
Elfer, P. & Dearnley, K. (2007) 'Nurseries and Emotional Well-being: Evaluating an Emotionally Containing Model of Professional Development'. *Early Years*. 27 (3) pp. 267–278.

Hawkins, P. & Shohet, R. (2012) *Supervision in the Helping Professions*. 4th edn. Maidenhead: McGraw-Hill, Open University Press.

Holland, P. (2003) *We Don't Play with Guns Here: War, Weapons and Superhero Play in the Early Years*. Maidenhead: Open University Press.

Hopkins, J. (1988) 'Facilitating the Development of Intimacy between Nurses and Infants in Day Nurseries'. *Early Child Development and Care*. 33 (1) pp. 99–111.

Inskipp, F. & Proctor, B. (1993) *The Art, Craft & Task of Counselling Supervision Part 1: Making the Most of Supervision*. Twickenham: Cascade Publications.

Inskipp, F. & Proctor, B. (2001) *Becoming a Supervisor*. London: Cascade.

Jackson, E. (2008) 'The Development of Work Discussion Groups in Educational Settings'. *Journal of Child Psychotherapy*. 34 (1) pp. 62–82.

Louis, S. (2017) 'Examining the Impact of a Discussion Group on the Self-perception of Early Years Practitioners.' Unpublished.

Manning-Morton, J. (2006) 'The Personal Is Professional: Professionalism and the Birth to Threes Practitioner'. *Contemporary Issues in Early Childhood*. 7 (1) pp. 42–52.

Implementing Work Group Supervision and bringing observational practice into focus using Work Group Supervision

This chapter has a twofold purpose. Firstly, it will discuss the importance of supporting Early Years educators in their role of noticing significant development and learning. The second purpose is to outline the roles, rights and responsibilities of the Early Years educators and the facilitator.

How Early Years educators feel is important

Work Group Supervision is not just concerned with what happens to infants and young children – it is also concerned with what happens to the Early Years educators working with them. Early Years educators are important people in a child's life. Children must feel safe and secure with them in order to learn many new things. Early Years educators have an important role to play in being continually supportive and encouraging in order for children to develop and progress. But who supports the Early Years educators to reflect on their knowledge and understanding about children?

As I have reiterated throughout this book, Early Years educators' observations of individual children are a fundamental part of their professional development and practice. Early Years educators need to know about the capabilities, strengths and weaknesses of the children that they are working with and this knowledge will come from observations. However, merely gathering information about a child through observing them is not enough. It is how Early Years educators use and interpret the information that makes the greatest difference to the children's future outcomes. It is not surprising that this area is the most neglected and requires the most support.

Supporting Early Years educators

Early Years educators may have many concerns about their work – these could include anything from not understanding how children learn to not being able to form an attachment with children; feeling disempowered and fearful; worrying about a child playing alone; gaining confidence in voicing their professional opinion; and achieving job satisfaction. It is how leaders and managers explore and support these concerns that will help to professionalise the workforce. Leaders and managers are in a position to assist Early Years educators by providing them with both time and space for sharing together, practising techniques, voicing opinions, making decisions and solving problems. Leaders and managers can also assist in the broader issues by trying to identify appropriate support or professional training and development. It is vital that leaders and managers understand the role of Work Group Supervision in helping Early Years educators to develop practice knowledge.

Work Group Supervision seeks to support Early Years educators to reflect on the information that comes from an observation as a whole group, discussing what they have noticed and understood. In this way, making the best use of what is known about children's learning will help plan to support it through providing linked learning experiences, so that children can practise and consolidate their skills. This will ensure that Early Years educators capture the unfolding developmental progress.

The lack of training and professional development opportunities available to Early Years educators has ultimately had a significant effect on the quality of care and education as well as confidence and morale. Without access to such training, professional development and understanding may not be enhanced. It is the responsibility of leaders and managers to probe the depth of Early Years educators' knowledge and understanding about the children they work with as well as supporting their professional development. Work Group Supervision is not just a tool for Early Years educators – it will also help leaders and managers better ensure that Early Years educators have sufficient knowledge and skills in supporting children's learning; have appropriate expectations for children's development and learning; are aware of the needs and abilities of children; are providing children with sufficient stimulation and challenge; and have sufficient knowledge of all curriculum areas of development and learning

A recent study by Melhuish and Gardiner (2019) shows how training matters for Early Years educators and the children that they teach. Melhuish (2019:12) notes: "A better staff-to-child ratio leads to improvements in quality, but staff qualifications and training is the most important factor." Their study finds that having well-trained and qualified staff increases the quality of care and education offered to children in the early years. This suggests that relevant training in child development – rather than a high level of formal education and adult-child ratios – has been found to be a major indicator of the quality of Early Years education. For these reasons, leaders and managers must work closely in supporting Early Years educators in providing the best possible care and education for the children that they work with as their interactions can affect the long-term outcomes for children.

How leaders and managers show support is important

One of the most important things that managers and leaders can do is to let Early Years educators know that they care about their professional development. Talking to Early Years educators about their children, exploring difficulties and creating an atmosphere where they feel able to talk, make suggestions and ask for help can contribute toward developing trusting and supportive relationships with staff.

Another important thing to note is how leaders and managers help Early Years educators to respond to their observations and follow through with learning activities that support children's interests. There will be a number of activities that Early Years educators can do confidently and independently with children. Sometime managers and leaders just need to point out the educational value of an experience. For example, many Early Years educators may read and tell stories to children but may not understand why this is important. Leaders and managers can help Early Years educators understand how important it is to encourage and support children in their care in what they try to do, not only what they can already do successfully, and share ways of doing this.

That said, leaders and managers will be aware that some Early Years educators may need support in how to write an observation, recognise significant learning, and use children's past learning experiences to build on future learning and development. Providing this kind of targeted support can be achieved through Work Group Supervision. Some Early Years educators, like the ones in my study, lacked confidence and knowledge and were intimidated by the process of observation. This had an impact on their sense of well-being, as well as their ability to enhance the children's experiences and learning development.

Within Work Group Supervision, leaders and managers can gain valuable insight into how Early Years educators are meeting children's developing needs; their styles of interacting; experiences that they are offering children; how the learning environment is responding to children interests; how learning is supported and linked to previous learning experiences; how children's interests are observed, supported and extended; and how they share knowledge of the children's development and learning with parents.

Work Group Supervision

Work Group Supervision underpins the very essence of quality care and education – without it Early Years educators cannot continuously develop their knowledge, techniques and abilities. It is the process of observing, understanding, recording and assessing that gives Early Years educators the knowledge and information that they need in order to support and plan ways of helping children to develop and learn. Work Group Supervision has an important role to play in supporting Early Years educators' well-being and observational practice, giving leaders and managers valuable insight into how Early Years educators interact with children.

This model of Continuing Professional Development seeks to improve the knowledge of Early Years educators about how children learn. Hawkins and Shohet (2012) note that "supervision can be an important part of taking care of oneself, staying open to new learning and an indispensable part of the individual's ongoing self-understanding, self-awareness and commitment to learning". It is essential to adopt a supervision approach which focuses on self-understanding and self-development through reflective peer group discussion. My research finds that when the Early Years educators present critical incidents for discussion, the process enables them to receive help and feedback on their techniques of observation while identifying children's individual needs, recognising their emotional reactions to their work, and reflecting on and challenging their assumptions, as well as receiving group support through a shared experience. Managers and leaders need to know what is important to Early Years educators concerning both their observations and the broader issues. In practice, Work Group Supervision allows for leaders and managers to work more closely with them to discuss, advise and support them when poor or superficial observation practice is identified. The strength of the Work Group Supervision is that it seeks to support the whole team to address practice issues through appropriate guidance before they spiral and become damaging to children and themselves.

Work Group Supervision has children's developing learning and the quality of interactions with Early Years educators as part of its primary purpose. It seeks to support the professional development of Early Years educators in understanding how children learn while increasing their levels of confidence. Work Group Supervision can help Early Years educators to learn more effectively by promoting teamwork and gives them more opportunities to practise observational practical skills and techniques. The group supervision is sufficiently flexible to be adapted to the needs of different levels of experience as its forms can be varied, though its functions remain focused on interpretations of observations, good quality adult interaction and professional development.

In the light of this, clear evidence from my research links Work Group Supervision to the quality of care and education and children's progress. It shows that this group supervision is most effective when its educational and supportive functions are separated from its managerial and evaluative functions. Work Group Supervision provides a number of ways for Early Years educators, leaders and managers to investigate and study the complexity of observations, understanding and interpretations, and encourages Early Years educators to question one another's professional practice in a supportive way. To be successful, the group supervision should also be externally led and focused on observation rather than externally imposed and centred on institutions.

Principles of Work Group Supervision

In developing a new model for Work Group Supervision, it is necessary to draw on guiding principles.

- It maintains and improves the quality of care and education
- It can apply to all Early Years educators regardless of their level of qualification
- Work Group Supervision is a vital aspect of contemporary Early Years practice and needs facilitators of sufficient expertise and experience to support educators
- Work Group Supervision should be held at least once every four weeks
- Work Group Supervision is an active problem-solving process between group members
- The facilitator is adequately prepared and experienced to be both critical and supportive

Getting started

Putting together a Work Group Supervision policy is a useful place to begin. The policy will need to have an emphasis on close observation of the child in order to understand and interpret their play. It will also prepare the Early Years educators for what will happen during the four staged parts of the process. The policy should include the setting's approach to Work Group Supervision and its aims and objectives, identify the group facilitator, and outline rights and responsibilities of both the facilitator and the group members. The main aim is to support Early Years educators to develop their knowledge and understanding of young children through reflection, discussion, research and observation. Responsibilities include:

- The Early Years educator taking responsibility for the observation that they present to the group for scrutiny and challenge
- The quality of the learning environment, experiences and interactions

- Taking part in professional dialogue and discussion with colleagues
- Observing significant development and learning
- Making judgements about how best to support, extend and enrich learning
- Reflecting on own practice
- Being open to discussing the impact of judgemental observations
- Commitment to active learning processes
- Be prepared to give and receive feedback to inform practice

Several other aspects can be included in the policy, such as the role of Work Group Supervision in supporting observation development. Close observations of children in Work Group Supervision allows Early Years educators to understand the capabilities of children as well as to gain insight into how and where children like to learn. Work Group Supervision should take place within work teams that are known to each other. The size of the group is also important. Eight to ten group members is ideal. This allows for smaller groups of two to four people to be formed throughout the session. If the sub-group is too large, of five people or more, some members might feel uncomfortable talking to it. One person in each small group shares with the whole group what they talked about.

Choosing a facilitator

It is important that the facilitator is engaged in the process and is neither judgemental or controlling. This is important because the facilitator will be expected to challenge practice. One of the major benefits of having an external facilitator is that it does not create issues with trust and respect in the group, which can affect the group dynamics. The role and responsibilities of the facilitator require them to be tuned in, to summarise the main points that have been discussed, and ask the group to move onto the next part of the process. It is important for everyone to be clear about why they are attending the Work Group Supervision, who the presenter is, and which child is up for discussion. Members of the group can agree the order of presenters together. They can also choose the child on who they will present. Responsibilities of the facilitator include:

- Motivating participants through each stage of the process
- Facilitating participants to learn together, share professional knowledge and reflect on their observational practice
- Informing Early Years educators about the Work Group Supervision
- Being open to participants' concerns or problems
- Showing initiative and enthusiasm throughout the process
- Recognising and appreciating the Early Years educator's starting point

- Building relationships with participants
- An ability to know how best to direct participants
- Addressing any roadblocks in the process
- Making and taking notes
- Being aware of the power dynamics
- Maintaining group confidentiality

Record-keeping

Records should be kept of what is discussed and any ideas and suggestions made. This includes judgements and understanding about children's learning. These records are not attributed to one individual but to the group's professional development file.

Frequency of Work Group Supervision

The group sessions with their individual presentations should take place every four to six weeks for an hour. This Work Group Supervision will involve discussion of an Early Years educator's presentation on observations of child-initiated learning and any key learning issues for the child. The setting will need to create a safe and comfortable space for Early Years educators to reflect on and discuss their work and their personal responses. It is best to arrange chairs in a circle so that the Early Years educators can participate and share ideas.

Burnout

Work Group Supervision helps Early Years educators to connect with their peers and develop self-awareness and self-understanding. Elfer and Dearnley (2007) are critical about the lack of support that some Early Years educators can get in preventing problems as well as the amount of help given to those who are struggling in their role.

In considering the benefits of Work Group Supervision, it needs to be made clear that it is not a therapy session, but a supportive group process. As the group facilitator I have helped and supported Early Years educators who are struggling with understanding children's developmental needs, who are working in isolation, lacking knowledge and confidence to support children's language development and fear making errors of judgement, all of which can cause or trigger burnout. Work Group Supervision has been shown to reduce burnout and increase emotional engagement and empowerment.

Continuing Professional Development for Early Years educators

Being able to present observations which demonstrate their skills and techniques enables Early Years educators to locate themselves in their practice and develop their understanding. Work Group Supervision provides Early Years educators with one dedicated hour a month to take part in group discussion designed to develop observational skills and understanding through reflection. The aim of the group supervision is to share the experience of observation, through reflection and discussion, which can enhance Early Years educators' knowledge and allow them to constantly reflect on this and their understanding about children, so that they are better equipped to support progress. The advantage of Work Group Supervision is that Early Years educators can support each other and teamwork is improved and promoted among staff. This can contribute to them feeling less isolated, give them a sense of belonging to a group, and improve communication. Importantly, Early Years educators are able to talk about difficult issues as well as challenging their own assumptions.

Finally, it may be concluded that providing effective supervision is key to promoting the emotional well-being of the Early Years workforce. It is through experiencing a supportive working environment that Early Years educators learn about themselves, children, and how best to respond and react to them. Implications for practice – we need to consider how we support Early Years educators theoretically and emotionally and at times of struggle.

Bringing observational practice into focus using Work Group Supervision

Work Group Supervision is based on the work of Hopkins (1988), Manning-Morton (2006), Elfer and Dearnley (2007) and Jackson (2008). This section explores ways in which Work Group Supervision can facilitate and guide observational processes and practice in Early Years settings. It will lead you to consider ways to support adults in developing their observation, pedagogy and practice and use case study examples to demonstrate the ways in which the supervision enables participants to develop their knowledge, observational skills and attitudes. The integrity of early childhood and children's need for protection – allowing them to develop holistically, uniquely and safely in family and community – lies at the centre of Work Group Supervision. It also addresses the need to support adults in their work with children and to develop and deepen their insights and understandings of the "what, why and how" of appropriate observation practice and pedagogy.

Supervision

As discussed in the previous chapter, supervision in Early Years settings is intended to improve the quality of job performance by supporting, coaching and empowering staff to meet responsibilities, exploring the emotional well-being of children and staff, contributing to protecting children and families, and developing pedagogical skills. It is also used to track training and development needs, review the effectiveness of the learning environment and staff interactions, and enhance children's learning and development.

Observation

Observation, central to effective Early Years practice, is at its best an active, meaningful task which stimulates thinking about what was seen, how to make changes to the environment to support and extend learning, and how to achieve outcomes. At worst, it is a passive and superficial exercise which misses significant development and can lead to over-reliance on checklists and developmental milestones, heightened fear and anxiety, and even complete burnout in the observer.

Friedrich Froebel in Lilley (1967) notes that observation of children requires adults to do more than just watch, but to listen carefully as well. Adults should be open-minded and curious about what the children are interested in. They should gain ideas from what they have observed and use these ideas to support children's play and learning. This means that adults need to know *how* to notice and do their utmost to understand the thoughts which children are incubating or exploring in their ideas and the ways in which children express their feelings individually and in relationships. According to Manning-Morton (2018:12), to do this successfully the Early Years educator needs to have "a thorough knowledge of a range of different theoretical perspectives on how infants and young children play, develop and learn. Where such knowledge is lacking, significant development will be missed". Clearly, the more knowledgeable that the Early Years educator is, the greater effect it can have on children's progress. Equally clear is how this meshes with Work Group Supervision and its primary function to enhance pedagogical knowledge and skills. Jackson (2008) recognises work group discussions as an important and rigorous professional activity which have the potential to help educators to develop and learn from their practice. The idea is to open up practice and allow the observer to come face-to-face with their own.

Work Group Supervision

Work Group Supervision offers managers, room leaders and supervisors the opportunity of enhancing pedagogical knowledge and skills. This is achieved through facilitating a structured discussion with a small group rather than having individual meetings. The group supervision can provide managers with a regular overview of how adults are supporting children to extend their learning, with the emphasis on the staff's understanding about their direct work and interactions with children. In this way Work Group Supervision draws on key components of supervision, including knowledge of how staff observe, interpret and respond to children. What matters deeply is how adults apply their professional knowledge and experience to their observations, which can have a significant impact on their ability to perform effectively.

The Work Group Supervision process begins with the Early Years educator presenting by reading his or her observation to the group. This is not dissimilar to what would already happen in supervision, where a manager might ask an Early Years educator to share their reflections about their performance. In the group supervision, Early Years educators share their initial thoughts about their observations only, talking freely on what is known about the child, while group members listen. This is important, because it can reveal what makes adults sit up and take notice.

Only the facilitator can ask questions, such as:

- What makes you say that?
- How much, and how well, do you think the child is learning?
- How do you think a change in the learning environment would support and extend learning?
- How could your interaction and support and extend learning?

The facilitator listens actively to the description of the child's learning. Next, the whole group thinks about and discusses what is already known about the child, including any prior learning, gaining insight into what is new or different about what the presenting adult has seen. Throughout this process the facilitator must be prepared to recognise and sensitively challenge the group's feelings and assumptions or lack of knowledge. The process is intended to help adults address any fears and anxieties about the content of the observation, whilst enhancing their pedagogical skills. Like supervision, Work Group Supervision can help to develop understanding and solve problems.

This first stage of Work Group Supervision is made up of two parts. The first is designed to uncover what knowledge adults bring to their observations and how open-minded they are about children's explorations, by requiring the presenting adult to relate to the group what they think is happening, making their interpretation public. Each stage of the group supervision encourages reflection at different levels. Unlike supervision on its own, Work Group Supervision does not focus on individual job performance – instead it emphasises support to improve whole staff performance. However, it is the responsibility of the facilitator to ask the presenting adult inquisitive questions, just as in supervision, in order to find the depth of the adult's knowledge. The next part of the first stage requires the presenting adult to work in a pair of their choosing to further interpret the observation and find understanding. It is also an opportunity to consider what assumptions they are making. This can give the presenting adult an insight into what children can do, what they might be interested in, their strengths, stage of development, and where they like to learn best. The ability to share one's thoughts and ideas about observations is an important professional activity. Work Group Supervision allows the presenting adults to make sense of these factors on a one-to-one basis, helping them to recognise what has been learnt by the child but also what possible changes they can make to their own future practice. One of the underpinning aims of this two-part process is to gain insight into significant thinking about observation practice through individual presentation, then discussion, then in pairs. Work Group Supervision is a valuable tool that helps adults recognise their own strengths and weaknesses. Providing time to think about how their observation practice has affected or enhanced children's development and learning is a helpful way to encourage reflection on their own knowledge and gain insight into the thinking and values in the professional practice of others.

In the second stage of the process, the pairs join another pair and work in a group of four. These groups reflect on the observation, considering in particular how they value play and learning and what assumptions they have made. Discussing the issues in the group, and then identifying ways to address or solve the problem, provides further opportunities for staff to develop and improve their pedagogical practice. The benefit of making observations public and discussing them in pairs and larger groups is that it allows insight from multiple perspectives. In this way Early Years educators will be sharing goals, knowledge and understanding, and developing relationships with each other.

The third stage of the process consists of the whole group discussing how well their initial thoughts match what is really happening, while also providing feedback and encouragement. Having time to reflect on children's emotional well-being and significant learning in their observations, to think about how they might engage in the situation differently, or make changes to the learning environment, is very important if these adults are to be relied upon to make judgements about children's development and learning. Clearly, managers of nurseries, kindergartens, pre-schools and crèches need to know what their staff are capable of so that they can form their own judgement about the setting's observational practice. Implementing the Work Group Supervision can certainly help managers to achieve this with all members of their team.

The fourth and final stage of the process involves the whole group supporting the presenting adult to evaluate what they now know and suggest strategies for implementation. This is a crucial stage – the process of evaluation allows Early Years educators to not only recognise their own levels of knowledge and understanding, but supports them to use a range of teaching and learning strategies with the children.

The second and third stages of the Work Group Supervision seek to develop pedagogical practice through focused feedback. By engaging in reflective conversations, Early Years educators become more responsive to each other's needs, beliefs and interests, and are more able to help each other. This is in line with the ideas of Vygotsky (1978), that by working together both the learners and more knowledgeable members of staff benefit from supporting each other to complete tasks. Another study shows that collaborative learning is not so much based on seeking the right answers, but about developing thinking that can lead to significant improvements in understanding. For example, Hanko (1999) concludes that teachers critically reflect when they collaborate on problems, showing that collaboration leads to understanding. This factor is found to have a more significant impact on understanding than any other, including in the Early Years educators' skillset. Farouk (2004) notes that the collaborative process is multifaceted. He suggests that during the processes of both discussion and reflection, the group discussions and questions can help toward reconstructing the teacher's self-understanding.

Receiving feedback is a central feature of the Work Group Supervision. Hawkins and Shohet (2012) explain that improvements are only minimal in the absence of supervision – simply directing staff in their practice may not necessarily lead to improvement or understanding. This assertion is consistent with Manning-Morton's findings (2006) from her model of Continuing Professional Development, focused on "relationship-based learning". One of the features encourages personal reflection on practice and theoretical thinking, resulting in sustained improvement. For feedback to be meaningful, it must be framed by meaningful learning experiences. For example, Early Years educators must reflect on a specific observation at different times during the Work Group Supervision process. Feedback would be specific to that stage as opposed to focusing on job performance.

Making one's observations public is not without challenge. Vulnerability can be present, not just in the process, but in the personal and professional attributes of the Early Years educators, especially concerning practice, or talking about practice, where they can feel like a novice, lacking in confidence and ability. The group discussions have the potential to contribute to a sense of well-being as Early Years educators begin to work with others on a similar journey. Consequently, opportunities to unpick observations and discuss effective teaching and learning are important for enhancing observational practice. If Early Years educators do not have opportunities to share knowledge with colleagues in the same setting it is likely that their understanding will be limited to personal knowledge, without developing new understanding about how children learn.

Although opportunities to discuss observational practice are not commonplace, they are necessary for Early Years educators. Bain and Barnett's (1986) summary of their work discussion group with Early Years educators notes that it helps staff to recognise their own feelings of inadequacy, struggle, and dislike of particular children, as well as reducing isolation. Similarly, Elfer (2012) notes that those taking part indicate that their participation helps them to engage with their emotional responses. This involves locating where these difficult feelings come from and understanding what they look like in practice. Notably, Elfer and Dearnley's article "Nurseries and Emotional Well-being" (2007) evaluates an emotionally containing model of professional development. This is where the group facilitators provide a model that is able to contain and support the difficult emotions that Early Years educators sometimes feel about their work. They say (2007:278):

> It needs to be recognised that resources have to be allocated for the time and facilitation for staff to think about and process the individual feelings evoked by their emotional work with the children. This also involves an attitudinal shift, seeing reflective practice as an entitlement of staff, both legitimate and necessary, if changes in professional practice are to be facilitated and sustained. Finally, the call for Early Years educators to have opportunities to discuss and reflect on their observational practice is consistent with discussion on professional development.

The facilitator

Work Group Supervision facilitation is an important and serious role and requires a depth of child development knowledge, skills and understanding to be effective. Managers who wish to implement Work Group Supervision should seek training in order to reflect on their own attitudes about supervising staff, their ability in supporting and directing staff practice, their own strengths and flaws, and areas that could be enhanced in delivering supervision. The success of Work Group Supervision depends on facilitation skills in leading the group, and the candidness of the facilitator to share and reflect effective practice. Successful facilitators should:

- Take an impartial position and focus simply on the group process and preferred outcomes
- Have a strategy for moving through each part of the process
- Pay close attention and ask questions that inspire and direct involvement applicable to the group's goals

- Ensure that all participants have a voice, sensitively drawing out quieter group members
- Embrace quietness and reflection
- Recognise when to contain the group's difficult emotions
- Support group collaboration by encouraging a shared understanding
- Retain the group focus on the task
- Be willing to listen candidly and share responsively
- Avoid dominating and/or following their own agenda
- Be thoughtful of the group members' individual and emotional needs

Clough and Nutbrown (2012:178) provide a useful methodological framework, in which they describe four forms of "radical enquiry", as radical looking, radical listening, radical reading and radical questioning. Radical looking relates to how the research process makes the familiar strange and exposes gaps in knowledge (2012:52); radical listening refers to the interpretive and critical ways in which the participant's voice is listened to (2012:63); radical reading outlines the critical task of taking on, or dismissing, existing knowledge and practices (2012:106); and radical questioning connects with the way in which "the research process acknowledges gaps in knowledge and locates the researcher's political motivations" (2012:140).

Acting as a group facilitator in the course of my research, the concepts of radical looking and radical listening were critical and significant. One of the aims is to try to balance power by listening to the participants. I used the Froebelian technique of being internally active and externally passive, which had an impact on how I observed, listened to and empathised with the participants, which led me to gear support to the Early Years educators' individual needs (Kaliala, 2005). In radical looking, this meant rigorously questioning the assumptions that I had taken for granted in relation to what I was seeing while minimising the impact of personal bias or power influences on the Work Group Supervision. Clough and Nutbrown's concept of radical listening and giving voice to the research experience are both related to that of empowerment. Indeed, while they are similar concepts in many respects, the concept of radical listening is particularly useful as it brings to notice the significance of my position and relationship within the research, as well as enhancing the aims.

Most importantly, the application of these concepts alerted and expanded my perception of the participant voice and I began to listen more carefully. The process of radical looking and radical listening made me more self-aware, in the sense that they provided theoretical clarity about giving a voice to participants, which, in turn, led to a heightened awareness of my own motivations influencing the Work Group Supervision.

Empowerment

Early Years educators are empowered when group discussions are facilitated so that they feel valued and encouraged to interpret their observations for themselves. For example, before the Work Group Supervision, the participants were not encouraged to make their own decisions about what they observed – they just followed the developmental descriptors outlined in the curriculum framework and this created a sense of disempowerment. After taking part in the discussions, the participants worked together and were able to question their own practice and make decisions about the children's learning.

Power and empowerment are defined as helping the participant to use and claim the powers available to them (Zimmerman, 1995). Within the Work Group Supervision power and empowerment are positioned within the social constructivist framework. From this perspective, power and empowerment are viewed as being different for each participant. They are governed by the socio-cultural and ecological context in which the participants interact and also as a collective knowledge base from which individual needs are addressed, and not from other sources of power. In other words, nothing else is taken into account other than what is presented to the group and learnt through interactions.

While it could be assumed that the facilitator has all the power, Early Years educators also have the power to say what they really feel, or not, or to say what they think the facilitator wants to hear. Empowerment of participants can be seen in how the facilitator supports them in the discussion and to question what underpins their practice, resulting in them becoming more reflective and responsive to the children. Throughout the process, the Early Years educators talk about their relationships with children and each other and how they are changing. This gives the facilitator valuable insight into how the process of talking about knowledge and understanding with colleagues and sharing their ideas can increase a sense of empowerment. In this regard, power and empowerment were dependent on how I interpreted the power and vulnerabilities of all participants' words and behaviour.

What are the challenges?

The perception of the term 'supervision' to many Early Years educators is that the process of the group discussion is hierarchical. Rather, it is a supportive and learning process that helps Early Years educators to develop professional practice and they should be encouraged to view it as such. If some Early Years educators feel insecure, emotionally unsupported, and sensitive to criticism, 'supervision' may cause a sense of fear and anxiety – they may believe that the sole purpose is to monitor their work performance. Other challenges can include a fear of exposure and fear of failure. They may also feel threatened and anxious about the safety of the process.

Given that the process of presenting observations to the group may be perceived as threatening to some Early Years educators, it follows that this may present a number of challenges for the facilitator. The first of these is ensuring that each member of the group is allocated time to reflect on, analyse and question their colleagues' observational work. Inspiring Early Years educators towards self-understanding requires facilitators to effectively manage each stage of the process, to ensure that all group members have an opportunity to have their emerging and changing perspectives articulated. This can be challenging when Early Years educators share inadequacies in understanding of child development, observational skills or professional/personal attitude. Self-understanding is a critical part of the Work Group Supervision process. It is important that facilitators carefully and purposefully follow the intended four-stage structure – however, this can be deeply challenging if facilitators lack experience. The Work Group Supervision can be fraught with uncertainty. Facilitators may have to deal with and contain painful or difficult emotions among the Early Years educators which have been evoked as a result of their work with children. Manning-Morton (2006) advises that when feelings are too painful to think about, we frequently defend ourselves psychologically by reacting in a way that denies or avoids them. Such emotions therefore need to be acknowledged and handled sensitively.

Other challenges may include facilitators themselves not having a detailed knowledge of how children learn. This is problematic – the functioning and dynamics of the group may be affected if facilitators are not knowledgeable about child learning, or if they do not have facilitation skills. Linked to this, facilitators also need to know what feedback they want from the group and they have to be prepared to challenge the members to critically reflect on and analyse their practice. But perhaps the most difficult challenge for facilitators is knowing when to step in and guide and when to step back, be observant and listen.

What are the benefits?

Many benefits flow from facilitating professional learning and development, with a focus on expanding observational skills, processes and practice. Learning from and with each other, learning from the experience of others, shared problem solving – all these come from being together as a work group, exploring the same observation from a number of different perspectives. In this sense, the group is on the same learning journey with each person at a different starting point.

The process of critical analysis and questioning of one's observational work in the Work Group Supervision, if done well, can lead to the group being a sounding board for helpful ideas about practice. Early Years educators also become more accountable to a broader community of learners. The development of new self-understanding has an impact on personal and professional growth – enabling Early Years educators to better locate themselves in their practice, realise their limitations and address them within the emotional security of the group supervision session. As a result, increasing individual knowledge and confidence is applied to everyday practice. Being able to better manage and contain anxiety leads to a practice enthused with meaningful emotional engagement and a quality of care for babies and young children. However, it would be a mistake to embrace the stance that observational work should be the sole measure of Early Years educators' job performance. While it is reasonable to assume that Work Group Supervision is certainly necessary within the Early Childhood sector, the ultimate criteria for effective observations must be children's development and learning. Anything else misses the point. With clear strategies in place for supporting Early Years educators to recognise and enhance children's learning, they can develop their professional practice.

The model of Work Group Supervision described in this chapter is not easily implemented. It requires a skilled and knowledgeable facilitator. It also requires a willingness on the part of the participants to recognise their inadequacies and a willingness to be part of the group discussions. Although my vision is ambitious, it is not new. Siraj-Blatchford (2010) asserts that training for Early Years educators lacks coherence and should not be the only way to support their development of knowledge. She recognises that other steps must be taken to support them.

Conclusion

Thus, as with any new model, Work Group Supervision will continue to develop, change and transform as Early Years educators gain experience and insight. Combining observational practice with Work Group Supervision is inherently empowering, enabling Early Years educators to expand their thinking and ideas about how children develop and learn, and in turn the impact on professional performance. However, we need to consider the implications to practice, specifically how we can support Early Years educators to sufficiently observe and respond to infants and young children; so that they can better understand the way that they are developing learning.

In this chapter we have looked at guidelines for implementing Work Group Supervision. The next chapter discusses the many different models of group consultation.

Bibliography

Bain, A. & Barnett, L. (1986) 'The Design of a Day Care System in a Nursery Setting for Children under Five'. *Document No. 2T347*. London, Tavistock Institute of Human Relations [TIHR].

Clough, P. & Nutbrown, C. (2012) *A Student's Guide to Methodology*. London: Sage Publication Ltd.

Elfer, P. (2012) 'Emotion in Nursery Work: Work Discussion as a Model of Critical Professional Reflection'. *Early Years: An International Research Journal*. 32 (2) pp. 129–141.

Elfer, P. & Dearnley, K. (2007) 'Nurseries and Emotional Well-being: Evaluating an Emotionally Containing Model of Professional Development'. *Early Years*. 27 (3) pp. 267–278.

Farouk, S. (1999) 'Consulting with Teachers'. *Educational Psychology in Practice: Theory, Research and Practice in Educational Psychology*. 14 (4) pp. 253–263.

Farouk, S. (2004) 'Group Work in Schools: A Process Consultation Approach'. *Educational Psychology in Practice Theory, Research and Practice in Educational Psychology*. 20 (3) pp. 207–220.

Froebel, F. W. (1887) *The Education of Man*. New York: Appleton.

Hanko, G. (1985) *Special Needs in Ordinary Classrooms: From Staff Support to Staff Development*. 3rd edn. London: David Fulton.

Hanko, G. (1999) *Increasing Competence through Collaborative Problem Solving: Using Insight into Social and Emotional Factors in Children's Learning*. London: D. Fulton Publishers.

Hawkins, P. & Shohet, R. (2012) *Supervision in the Helping Professions*. 4th. Maidenhead: McGraw-Hill, Open University Press.

Hopkins, J. (1988) 'Facilitating the Development of Intimacy between Nurses and Infants in Day Nurseries'. *Early Child Development and Care*. 33 (1) pp. 99–111.

Inskipp, F. & Proctor, B. (1993) *The Art, Craft & Task of Counselling Supervision Part 1: Making the Most of Supervision*. Twickenham: Cascade Publications.

Inskipp, F. & Proctor, B. (2001) *Becoming a Supervisor*. London: Cascade.

Jackson, E. (2008) 'The Development of Work Discussion Groups in Educational Settings'. *Journal of Child Psychotherapy*. 34 (1) pp. 62–82.

Kaliala, M. (2005) *Play Culture in a Changing World*. Maidenhead: Open University Press.

Lilley, I. M. (1967) *Friedrich Froebel. A Selection from His Writing*. Cambridge: Cambridge University Press.

Manning-Morton, J. (2006) 'The Personal Is Professional: Professionalism and the Birth to Threes Practitioner'. *Contemporary Issues in Early Childhood*. 7 (1) pp. 42–52.

Manning-Morton, J. (2018) 'Noticing, Recognising, Responding and Reflecting: The Process of Observing Infants and Young Children'. *Early Education Journal*. 85 pp. 11–13.

Melhuish, E. (2019) 'Training Matters.' *Nursery World*. May 2019, p. 12.

Melhuish, E. & Gardiner, J. (2019) 'Structural Factors and Policy Change as Related to the Quality of Early Childhood Education and Care for 3–4 Year Olds in the UK'. *The Journal Frontiers in Education*. 4 pp. 1–15.

Proctor, B. (1997) 'Contracting in Supervision'. In: Sills, C. (ed) *Contracts in Counselling*. pp. 190–206. London: Sage.

Proctor, B. (2008) *Group Supervision: A Guide to Creative Practice*. London. Sage.

Siraj-Blatchford, I. (2010) 'Learning in the Home and at School: How Working-Class Children Succeed against the Odds'. *British Educational Research Journal*. 36 (3) pp. 463–482.

Soni, A. (2013) 'Group Supervision: Supporting Practitioners in Their Work with Children and Families in Children's Centres'. *Early Years: An International Research Journal*. 33 (2) pp. 146–160.

Steel, L. (2001) 'Staff Support through Supervision'. *Emotional and Behavioural Difficulties*. 6 (2) pp. 91–101.

Vygotsky, L. S. (1978) *Mind and Society: The Development of Higher Mental Processes*. Cambridge, MA: Harvard University Press.

Zimmerman, B. J. (1995) 'Self-Efficacy and Educational Development'. In: Bandura, A. (ed) *Self-Efficacy in Changing Societies*. pp. 202–231. New York: Cambridge Univ. Press.

7 | Group consultation

The group consultation approach is about a professional consultant working with a group as opposed to an individual. Each session is facilitated by the same experienced consultant and follows a set of processes, depending on the approach. Group consultation provides attendees with opportunities to examine their own work and that of others; solve problems; apply new learning; gain insight into other people's perspectives; and discuss their struggles and difficulties with work among the group. More and more, group consultation is emerging as a sustainable and crucial way in which whole teams can be supported to acquire knowledge and refine understanding. The term group consultation is often used to describe professional development activities where groups of people in the same profession meet regularly with one or two consultants to discuss work-related issues. While there are many different models of group consultation, they have more similarities than they have differences.

Group consultation approaches which help educators and teachers to develop their professional practice have been used effectively in schools. However, in the course of my research I could not find anyone who had applied Vygotsky's concept of the Zone of Proximal Development (ZPD) to adults. Traditionally, ZPD has been applied to children in education settings to describe the development which a learner can achieve independently and with guidance. I have had several discussions with colleagues and education psychologists, who agree that ZPD can be applied to learning situations, not just for children but for adults as well. In this chapter I draw upon various approaches to establish links between Vygotsky's theoretical frameworks and group consultation processes.

Interestingly, Zuckerman (2007:51) states:

> For adults, the task of constructing a meeting with the child on the territory of play, learning activity, or directly emotional or intimate personal communication

is always a new task, however experienced the adult may be in solving similar tasks. The task is new for the adult for he is seeking for the first time a method of adjusting his action to the action of this specific child in such a way that something new should arise at the place where the two actions meet.

In other words, these are situations in which both participants are creating the Zone of Proximal Development for each other. Zuckerman seems to imply that such a meeting with a child always demands that a teacher act in the zone of their own proximal development.

I wanted to expand Vygotsky's ZPD to include collaboration between Early Years educators as a vehicle of continuing professional development of Observation, Assessment and Planning (OAP) skills. Starting from this perspective, I have constructed a particular form of Continuing Professional Development (CPD) which draws heavily upon Vygotsky's ideas. It is also influenced by several models of group and process consultation including Schein's (1987) ideas about effective communication and the development of interpersonal skills, and the centrality given to the educative aspect of group supervision taken by Hanko (1999).

In many respects, Vygotsky places much emphasis on the role of a collective society in sharing knowledge and skills. According to Vygotsky (1978), he suggests that many of the discoveries which learners make happen in collaborative dialogue with a skilful tutor. Vygotsky claims that students learn more effectively when working with others – it is through such collaboration with those who are more experienced that students learn to internalise new concepts. Vygotsky (1978:86) defines the Zone of Proximal Development as "the distance between the actual development level as determined by independent problem-solving and the level of potential development as determined through problem-solving under adult guidance or in collaboration with more capable peers".

In Vygotsky's view, collaborative learning is more likely to occur within the learner's ZPD and guidance should be targeted there. He sees development and learning as being influenced by dialogue and discussion with others in a social context. In his view, working together with peers in collaborative social situations gives the learner sufficient opportunity to observe and develop their own performance, which they would not benefit from alone. Chaiklin (2003) explains that collaborative endeavours are not only about the adult being more knowledgeable than the student but are also about the adult's understanding of the student's thinking. Chaiklin (2003:11) argues that the term "collaboration" relates to situations where the learner is offered some interaction with another person in relation to the problem being solved.

I used ZPD as a guide to determine the gap between the expected level of skill and knowledge as put forward by the Tickell Review (2011) and the actual practice of the participants in my study, to determine what support was needed. I wanted the participants to engage in recall and reflection in pairs and group discussions to deepen their understanding of observation and implementation. Managers in the area where I carried out my study had identified significant gaps in their Early Years educators' knowledge of the OAP process. The significance of this gap between what was expected, and actual practice, justified the need for a more sensitive approach than the official one of supporting the Early Years educators' development and needs.

I set out with the assumption that professional development has to be meaningful for Early Years educators and supportive of their development and practice for it to be truly effective. Two elements were needed to form part of my support – subjectivity, which describes the process of where the participants begin with different understanding and experiences, and intersubjectivity, which explores the interactions that take place during the collaborative problem process.

Vygotsky's social constructivist perspective

Vygotsky's (1978) theory is based on the idea that human beings develop intellectually independent cultural characteristics by joining in cultural activities and then internalising the meanings of that activity. This process is founded on the notion that culture produces mediated means which represent internalised meaning and allow the individual to behave in culturally relevant ways. In elaborating his theory, Vygotsky claims that individuals are capable of functioning at higher intellectual levels when they work collaboratively rather than individually. Vygotsky is concerned with the interaction between learners during joint activity – he states that "every function in the child's cultural development appears twice, first on a social level and later on an individual level, first between people and then inside the child" (1978:57). This definition implies that the higher functions start off as the relationship between learners.

From this perspective, learning is a social process that involves receiving guidance and/or support from a more knowledgeable other, who has a better understanding or greater ability in respect to a particular task, process or concept. Language is identified as an important cultural tool which serves to move learning from the social to the individual level. Vygotsky considers the role of the adult to be vital in guiding learners with tasks which are just ahead of their current ability. With such guidance, he asserts, the learner can function ahead of their own capacity. Vygotsky uses the Zone of Proximal Development to define the distance between the learner's ability to perform a task under adult guidance, and/or peer collaboration, and the learner's ability to solve the problem independently. This definition suggests that guidance should be directed at supporting maturing functions rather than functions which the learners have already achieved.

Another aspect of his theory considers joint understanding as central in developing higher levels of thinking. Vygotsky (1978:87) highlights the importance of a shared dialogue in collaborative activities in enhancing learning. He states that learners can "perform … in collaboration with one other that which they have not mastered independently". He also asserts that collaboration brings about a shared understanding of the problem as a result of the learner, and more knowledgeable other, taking account of each other's perspective.

Implications of Vygotsky's constructivist theory on group consultation processes

Caplan (1970) defines consultation as:

> a process of interaction between two professional persons – the consultant, who is a specialist, and the consultee, who invokes the consultant's help regarding a current work problem, which he or she has decided is within the other's area of specialised competence.

This definition implies that consultation is both a collaborative and directed process, which involves learning on the part of the learner and the group facilitator. Ideally, the learner develops in areas where there have previously been difficulties and the facilitator learns the level of support needed by the pupil. Vygotsky (1978) offers a powerful theoretical framework in which the role of culture and social learning is viewed as a central tenet.

Vygotsky asserts that learning is a process which involves the pupil being actively engaged. Knowledge cannot merely be transferred but is constructed through joint meaningful activity. This aspect of his theory can be seen to relate to both the group facilitator (consultant) and learner (consultee), as both will develop new knowledge and understanding of the issues being explored. Another aspect of Vygotsky's theory which can be translated to group consultation is that of joint understanding. Vygotsky views language and dialogue as one of many cultural tools for enhancing learning. His problem-solving approach establishes important links between collaborative dialogue in group consultations and collaborative problem solving between learners (Caplan, 1970). Indeed, both approaches provide opportunities for the learner to listen to the perspective of others as they reflect on their practice. This link between problem solving and group consultation is further articulated by the importance placed on problem solving in both approaches. Vygotsky's emphasis on the learner engaging in collaborative activities to learn from others could also relate to the thoughtful interactions during the group consultation process between the facilitator and the participants.

Problem-solving approaches to group consultation

Definitions of group consultation tend to focus upon the type of intervention needed to support the situation. Caplan (1970) developed a model of Mental Health Consultation with a number of overlapping features:

- Client-centred case consultation
- Consultee-centred case consultation
- Programme-centred administrative consultation
- Consultee-centred administrative consultation

Caplan recommends that the consultee-centred model should be offered to professionals with a psychodynamic approach, which utilises the need for collaborative dialogue to bring about reflection. The aim is to give professionals a space to discuss problems with a consultant, paying close attention to what others in the group say, and reflect on their practice. He argues that this process increases self-awareness and knowledge of possible solutions to address a problem. This is echoed by Schon (1983), who views reflection as a way to support teachers to develop their practice. The literature suggests that the reflective process can help professionals engage in developing knowledge, skills and understanding. It also establishes a link with Vygotsky's Zone of Proximal Development, indicating the relationship between the consultant and consultee, the consultant's understanding of the consultee's difficulty, and their ability to help the consultee learn. The link is made more explicit by the collaborative problem-solving process between professionals.

Hanko (1999) promotes a psychodynamic and systemic thinking approach which gives priority to collaborative relationships between the consultant, group and school. Hanko's (1999:9) definition of the consultant's role differs from Caplan (1970), as Hanko's view is that consultants should not present as experts – rather, they should act as "a non-directive facilitating fellow professional skilled in the art of sharing his experience and expertise in a process of joint exploration of a problem". Hanko's (1999:32) approach asks teachers thoughtful "answerable questions" about the difficulties they are experiencing. Hanko (1999:61) says that the collaborative process allows teachers to advance their knowledge and skills and is therefore able to "reinstate a sense of 'objectivity' to the situation". However, Bozic and Carter (2002) and Farouk (2004) argue that Hanko's view does not accommodate the teacher's personal agenda, bias and emotional needs. As such, this can affect the successful functioning of the group. Both Vygotsky (1978) and Bronfenbrenner (1979) recognise that these factors play a crucial role in human development. Bronfenbrenner identifies four interacting systems which he says have an influence on children's interactions and relationships. He presents these as a framework of interacting forces for understanding how individual or group processes are affected by environmental systems in which they function.

- The Microsystem relates to indirect and direct interpersonal relationships with the child.
- The Mesosystem relates to the connections between the relationships of the child's microsystems.
- The Exosystem is concerned with the structures which the child does not have direct contact with but is influenced by (policy and practice).
- The Macrosystem is influenced by culture and child-rearing traditions and beliefs.

Vygotsky's ZPD considers the role of relationships in the child's microsystem. Here the microsystem represents the social and cultural factors and emphasises the role of the adult. He argues that interaction is beneficial to the learner when another, who knows more about the task, assists. The more knowledgeable other benefits too, as the process of collaboration helps to bring a sense of objectivity to what is known. This last point relates to Hanko's claim that collaboration enhances learning and can enable interpersonal experiences to be transformed into intrapersonal competence.

My approach builds on that of Hanko by asking Early Years educators a series of thoughtful questions which focus them on their observations. Farouk (2004) outlines a four-stage solution-focused approach, based on combining the ideas from Hanko and Schein's (1987) Process Consultation model. Farouk's approach aims at providing opportunities for teachers to reflect on and develop their personal ideas and support practice through generating new strategies. Farouk reports several advantages – teachers are given space to reflect on their interactions with the children, they feel that they gain a deeper understanding of the children's needs, and that they can better support children in achieving goals. Farouk's approach resonates with Vygotsky's assumptions that the learner's development can only be understood in the social context, thus, interpersonal factors should not be separated from that context.

Wilson and Newton (2006) developed a ten-stage process called Circles of Adults (CoA), which incorporates group consultation with graphic facilitation. This approach draws heavily on that of Hanko's described earlier. According to Wilson and Newton, CoA processes have five main aims. These are:

- Collective problem solving
- Reflection
- An examination of the effect of organisational factors
- Emotional support
- Group feedback

Wilson and Newton's approach is intended to support adults working with children who have emotionally challenging behaviour. The aim is to develop a deeper understanding of a child or young person and to develop a set of hypotheses and strategies which better contain unmet learning and emotional needs. However, Bennett and Monsen (2011) criticise this approach as lacking in evaluation of interventions and strategies. Nonetheless, they assert that the structure is easy to access, and the materials may support possible group problem-solving processes.

Benefits and weaknesses of group consultation

The preceding literature offers insight into group consultation and the different processes which consultants focus on as a tool to enhance professional development. Caplan's (1970) approach has been particularly influential – many scholars have drawn on his psychodynamic model for their work with school-based consultations. Perhaps the most important aspect of this model is that it seeks to improve job performance, with a principal focus on helping clients gain insight as to how their personal feelings and behaviour may contribute to the presenting issues. The main aim of the consultant is to improve the clients' understanding of the difficult work issues and to increase their capacity to deal with them now or in the future.

A limitation rather than a weakness is that this consultation model has perhaps advanced beyond Caplan's original concept. Factors such as Bronfenbrenner's (1979) ecology theory and Vygotsky's socio-cultural theory of development, i.e. ZPD – both widely used in education – might offer consultants an alternative perspective, since they seek to understand the interactions between the individual and their environment. In my opinion, Caplan pays little attention to the socio-economic and political factors that may well contribute to an individual's ability to develop high mental functions.

Similarly, Hanko's (1999) approach gives little or no consideration to a school's culture or, indeed, the interactions that arise within a group (Farouk, 2004). However, its major strength is that it can help teachers to change fundamental beliefs about their practice by providing a space for reflective dialogue and discussion, where teachers feel that they have support and guidance. This last point establishes links with Vygotsky's claim that the construction of a shared language supports learning. Farouk's (2004) model combines group consultation with process consultation in order to attend to emotional and interpersonal factors. Like Vygotsky, Farouk considers the culture of the group, and personal characteristics of the participants, that could affect its dynamics. Perhaps this also shows how Vygotsky's constructivist frameworks might offer group consultation a more coherent approach. Meanwhile, Wilson and Newton's (2006) approach incorporates psychodynamics with group supervision and recognises the important role that group dynamics have.

This approach considers the importance of both reflection and feedback, while also recognising the effect of group dynamics. Vygotsky recognises social and cultural factors may influence collaborative learning which, in turn, may influence learning at an individual level.

Psychoanalytic approaches

Bain and Barnett's (1986) approach is based upon psychoanalytic theory and the social defences which organisations construct against emotional attachment to children. This is a highly particular model of work discussion and the first to offer support to Early Years educators. It centres on facilitating the development of relationships between Early Years educators and children, offering them weekly group sessions to talk about their relationships and experiences. Bain and Barnett report that the work discussions help staff to recognise their own feelings of inadequacy, struggle, and dislike of particular children. Elfer (2014:108) argues that the aim of this group is for participants to learn from "rigorous discussion of experience" with facilitators to achieve careful exploration of difficult issues.

Hopkins (1988) promotes an approach which advocates no teaching of any kind. This aims to provide support to Early Years educators through work discussions, in which they can express their personal and professional views about their attachment relationships with children. Facilitators attend to the unconscious feelings and anxieties of the group. Trained therapists predominantly use this model. These kinds of CPD groups have been criticised by teachers for failing to offer an immediate solution about how they should be working (Jackson, 2002). The argument of Manning-Morton (2006), that Early Years educators need professional reflection time which allows them to consider personal emotions in their professional practice, points to the potential benefits of work discussions in supporting this.

Elfer and Dearnley (2007) propose a particular model of support as a form of professional supervision, following their study based upon psychoanalytic theory with a group of 12 nursery heads. Elfer and Dearnley (2007:268) draw on the concept of "social defence systems" to explain the defence strategies which Early Years educators may use when certain aspects of their work become too emotionally difficult to deal with. Their approach offers facilitated support, in which attachment relationships and the emotional aspect of teaching and learning can be more thoughtfully explored and delicately challenged. They report many positive benefits and outcomes – the heads valued being able to discuss and share experiences, becoming more aware of what was happening in their nurseries. The heads also reported increased interaction and felt listened to and supported. One of the key aspects of this approach is the opportunity for Early Years educators to discuss and think about how they respond to the emotional demands of children. The concept of work discussions is directly linked to intersubjectivity between the participants and the facilitator and between the participants themselves and Vygotsky's notion of receiving help from a more knowledgeable other.

Subsequent research by Elfer (2012) and Page and Elfer (2013) advances Elfer and Dearnley's (2007) emphasis on work discussions as a tool for supporting the challenges encountered by Early Years educators as they engage with the emotions of young children. The aim of the work discussions is to support managers to critically reflect on their own emotional experiences. The facilitator does not decide what is discussed but keeps the discussions on task. Elfer (2012) reports that those taking part indicated that their participation allowed them to engage with their emotional responses and become more aware of the emotional context of their management experience. This led some of them to report feelings of guilt. Elfer argues that Early Years educators "should have an opportunity to talk through the emotional demands of such work". Davis and Ryder (2016:133) acknowledge that reflective discussions are a fundamental aspect of the manager's role. However, they warn that this type of work discussion relies completely on trust being established within the group and some settings may need to address this issue first.

Benefits and weaknesses of psychoanalytic approach

The work discussions approach is highly influenced by psychoanalytic insights and places a strong emphasis on providing Early Years educators with time to explore the emotional aspects of their role. Whilst Bain and Barnett's (1986) approach is pioneering in working with Early Years educators, it is costly to administer, which may discourage some PVI settings from using it. Despite this, the work of Bain and Barnett (1980), Hopkins (1988) and Elfer and Dearnley (2007) continues to inform the key person approach utilised in England's EYFS. Work discussion is used in professional support with trained facilitators and the advantages include:

- Change of perception (Bain & Barnett, 1986).
- Becoming more aware of children's individual needs (Bain & Barnett, 1986; Hopkins, 1988; Elfer & Dearnley, 2007; Elfer, 2012).
- Thoughtful observations (Hopkins, 1988; Elfer & Dearnley, 2007; Elfer, 2012).
- More responsive to the children (Bain & Barnett, 1986; Hopkins, 1988; Elfer & Dearnley, 2007; Elfer, 2012).
- More able to deal with children's difficult emotions (Bain & Barnett, 1986; Hopkins, 1988; Elfer & Dearnley, 2007; Elfer, 2012).

- Valuing the CPD and valuing being able to discuss and share experiences (Bain & Barnett, 1986; Hopkins, 1988; Elfer & Dearnley, 2007; Elfer, 2012).
- Becoming more aware of what is happening in their nurseries (Bain & Barnett, 1986; Elfer, 2012).
- Increased interaction (Elfer & Dearnley, 2007).
- Opportunity for reflection (Elfer & Dearnley, 2007; Elfer, 2012).
- Listened to and supported (Elfer & Dearnley, 2007; Elfer, 2012).

Negative impacts reported are:

- Not enough time allocated for group members to become more familiar with each other (Elfer, 2012).
- Initial feelings of anxiety about the model of CPD and that some group members do not participate (Hopkins, 1988; Elfer & Dearnley, 2007; Elfer, 2012).

Process Consultation

Schein (1987) describes a model of Process Consultation to help organisations make changes. He defines this approach as "a set of activities on the part of the consultant that helps the client to perceive, understand and act upon the process events that occur in the client's environment in order to improve the situation as defined by the client" (Schein, 1987:11). This approach is concerned with problem solving and supporting the consultee to find related appropriate solutions to their difficulties. The main aim is for the consultant to reveal the client's thinking and facilitate decision-making processes. This allows the consultee to take ownership of the problem to bring about change.

This is echoed by the argument of Reddy (1994), that the consultant should intervene no more than is necessary to meet the client's goals. Schein advocates active engagement on the side of the client which, he argues, is one of the main mechanisms to help them become more skilled in interpersonal communication and reaching their desired goal. This links to Vygotsky's (1978) assertion that members of an organisation can learn and change their behaviour based on support that they receive from others, moving beyond their current capability while still being within their potential (i.e. the Zone of Proximal Development).

Manning-Morton (2006) explains "process-oriented" (as a form of professional learning) to be based upon "andragogical problem base and collaborative perspective to adult learning", used to explain the importance of self-knowledge. This approach aims to support the Early Years educators' relationships with young children and is intended to promote their professional identity by encouraging critical reflection about the impact of their personal beliefs on their practice.

Benefits and weaknesses of Process Consultation

Schein's (1987) Process Consultation model pays attention to the development of the client's identity and interactions and includes external factors which may affect the client's involvement in the process. The strength of this approach is collaboration. This is essential to finding solutions, leading to the development of shared values and increased levels of self and group responsibility. Schein's approach is also both remedial and preventive – it seeks to develop the client's problem-solving skills, not to give out solutions. As far as weakness is concerned, his approach is dependent on an individual consultant's ability to reflect on his or her own behaviour – to know if they are giving clients answers or supporting them to find their own solutions. Despite the weaknesses, PC consultants try to give insight into "process events" (Schein, 1987:11).

Manning-Morton's (2006) approach has a strong evidence-based practice theory underpinning it. Manning-Morton (2006:44) claims that her model has led to "increased professional self-confidence, with respect to articulating their practice philosophy". It should be recognised, however, that the commitment needed from participants may hinder its use in some settings. Despite this, the model provides further emphasis on the importance of reflecting on personal emotions in professional practice, underpinned by a process-orientated approach to bring about changes.

This review of literature suggests that consultation, work discussions, or Work Group Supervision have the potential of supporting and developing Early Years educators' practice. I have argued that the Vygotskyian theoretical framework offers a complementary perspective which can be used by all the theoretical approaches. With so much emphasis on collaboration and interaction within the group consultation and work discussion approaches, it becomes evident that links are established with Vygotsky's notion of joint activity, which also seeks to build on the learner's own understanding.

However, Process Consultation, by the very nature of its focus on the development of the interactions between consultant and client, also lends itself to be applied to a Vygotskyian theoretical framework. Facilitating Early Years educators to develop their knowledge within a group context is particularly important, given that this can lead to them becoming more thoughtful about their practice (Manning-Morton, 2006; Elfer, 2014).

Conclusion

Overall the group consultation models of supervision reviewed in this chapter are not mutually exclusive, they share many common characteristics. The models attend systemically to establishing external facilitators, safe relationships, task-directed structures, problem-solving tasks, methods addressing practice issues, reflecting on and in practice, communication skills enhancing listening, analysing and collaboration. It is important to consider how these models change and transform professional practice and in turn impact on the emotional well-being of the Early Years educators.

In this chapter we have talked widely about group consultation. The next chapter examines the impact of Work Group Supervision on practice.

Bibliography

Bain, A. & Barnett, L. (1980) *The Design of a Day Care System in a Nursery Setting for Children under Five*. London: Tavistock Institute for Human Relations.

Bain, A. & Barnett, L. (1986) 'The Design of a Day Care System in a Nursery Setting for Children under Five', *Document No. 2T347*. London, Tavistock Institute of Human Relations [TIHR].

Bennett, S. & Monsen, J. J. (2011) 'A Critical Appraisal of Four Approaches Which Support Teachers' Problem Solving within Educational Settings'. *Educational Psychology in Practice*. 27 (1) pp. 19–35.

Bozic, N. & Carter, A. (2002) 'Consultation Groups: Participants' Views'. *Educational Psychology in Practice*. 18 (3) pp. 189–203.

Bronfenbrenner, U. (1979) *The Ecology of Human Development*. Cambridge, MA: Harvard University Press.

Bronfenbrenner, U. (1992) 'Ecological Systems Theory'. In: Vasta, R. (ed) *Six Theories of Child Development: Revised Formulations and Current Issues*. pp. 187–249. London: Jessica Kingsley.

Caplan, G. (1970) *The Theory and Practice of Mental Health Consultation*. New York: Basic Books.

Chaiklin, S. (2003) 'The Zone of Proximal Development in Vygotsky's Analysis of Learning and Instruction'. In: Kozulin, A., Gindix, B., Ageyev, V. S., & Miller, S. M. (eds) *Vygotsky's Educational Theory in Cultural Context*. pp. 39–63. Cambridge, UK: Cambridge University Press.

Davis, G. & Ryder, G. (2016) *Leading in Early Childhood*. New York: Sage.

Elfer, P. (1996) 'Building Intimacy in Relationships with Young Children in Nurseries'. *Early Years*. 16 (2) pp. 30–34.

Elfer, P. (2005) 'Observation Matters'. In: Abbott, L. & Langston, A. (eds) *Birth to Three Matters*. pp. 116–129. Maidenhead: Open University Press.

Elfer, P. (2006) 'Exploring Children's Expressions of Attachment in Nursery'. *European Early Childhood Research Journal*. 14 (2) pp. 81–95.

Elfer, P. (2007) 'Babies and Young Children in Nurseries: Using Psychoanalytic Ideas to Explore Tasks and Interactions'. *Children and Society*. 21 (2) pp. 111–122.

Elfer, P. (2009) *Life at Two: Attachments, Key People and Development*. Newcastle upon Tyne: Siren Films Ltd.

Elfer, P. (2012) 'Emotion in Nursery Work: Work Discussion as a Model of Critical Professional Reflection'. *Early Years: An International Research Journal*. 32 (2) pp. 129–141.

Elfer, P. (2013) 'Emotional Aspects of Nursery Policy and Practice – Progress and Prospect'. *European Early Childhood Education Research Journal*. 4 pp. 1–16.

Elfer, P. (2014) 'Social Defences in Nurseries'. In: Armstrong, D. & Rustin, M. J. (eds) *Social Defences against Anxiety: Explorations in the Paradigm*. Tavistock Clinic Series. pp. 284–299. London: Karnac.

Elfer, P. & Dearnley, K. (2007) 'Nurseries and Emotional Well-Being: Evaluating an Emotionally Containing Model of Professional Development'. *Early Years*. 27 (3) pp. 267–278.

Elfer, P., Goldschmied, E., & Selleck, D. (2003) *Key Persons in the Nursery: Building Relationships for Quality Provision*. London: David Fulton Publishers.

Elfer, P., Goldschmied, E., & Selleck, D. (2012) *Key Persons in the Early Years: Building Relationships for Quality Provision in Early Years Settings and Primary Schools*. 2nd edn. London: David Fulton.

Evans, S. (2005) 'The Development of a Group Consultation Approach to Service Delivery'. *Educational Psychology in Practice*. 21 (2) pp. 131–147.

Farouk, S. (1999) 'Consulting with Teachers'. *Educational Psychology in Practice: Theory, Research and Practice in Educational Psychology*. 14 (4) pp. 253–263.

Farouk, S. (2004) 'Group Work in Schools: A Process Consultation Approach'. *Educational Psychology in Practice Theory, Research and Practice in Educational Psychology*. 20 (3) pp. 207–220.

Farouk, S. (2014) 'From Mainstream School to Pupil Referral Unit: A Change in Teachers' Self-Understanding'. *Teachers and Teaching: Theory and Practice*. 20 (1) pp. 19–31.

Fleer, M. & Richardson, C. (2004) 'Mapping the Transformation of Understanding'. In: Anning, A., Cullen, J., & Fleer, M. (eds) *Early Childhood Education*. pp. 130–144. London, Thousand Oaks, CA, New Delhi: Sage.

Fleer, M. & Robbins, J. (2007) 'A Cultural-Historical Analysis of Early Childhood Education: How Do Teachers Appropriate New Cultural Tools?'. *European Early Childhood Research Journal*. 15 (1) pp. 103–119.

Fosnot, C. (1992) 'Constructing Constructivism'. In: Duffy, T. M. & Jonassen, D. H. (eds) *Constructivism and the Technology of Instruction*. pp. 167–176. Hillsdale, NJ: Lawrence Erlbaum Associates.

Fosnot, C. (ed) (2005) *Constructivism: Theory, Perspectives, and Practice*. 2nd edn. New York: Teachers College Press.

Gray, P. (2002) *Working with Emotions: Responding to the Challenge of Difficult Pupil Behaviour in Schools*. London: Routledge/Falmer.

Hanko, G. (1985a) *Special Needs in Ordinary Classrooms: From Staff Support to Staff Development*. 3rd edn. London: David Fulton.

Hanko, G. (1985b) *Special Needs in Ordinary Classrooms*. Oxford: Blackwell Education.

Hanko, G. (1999) *Increasing Competence through Collaborative Problem Solving: Using Insight into Social and Emotional Factors in Children's Learning*. London: D. Fulton Publishers.

Hanko, G. (2002) 'The Emotional Experience of Teaching: A Priority for Professional Development'. In: Gray, P. (ed) (2002). *Working with Emotions: Responding to the Challenge of Difficult Pupil Behaviour in Schools*. pp. 25–36. London: Routledge/Falmer.

Hopkins, J. (1988) 'Facilitating the Development of Intimacy between Nurses and Infants in Day Nurseries'. *Early Child Development and Care*. 33 (1) pp. 99–111.

Jackson, E. (2002) 'Mental Health in Schools – What about the Staff? Thinking about the Impact of Work Discussion Groups in School Settings'. *Journal of Child Psychotherapy*. 28 (2) pp. 129–146.

Jackson, E. (2008a) 'The Development of Work Discussion Groups in Educational Settings'. *Journal of Child Psychotherapy*. 34 (1) pp. 62–82.

Jackson, E. (2008b) *Work Discussion Groups at Work: Applying the Method in Work Discussion, Learning from Reflective Practice in Work with Children and Families*. The Tavistock Clinic Series. London: Karnac Books.

Manning-Morton, J. (2006) 'The Personal Is Professional: Professionalism and the Birth to Threes Practitioner'. *Contemporary Issues in Early Childhood*. 7 (1) pp. 42–52.

Newton, C. (1995) 'Circles of Adults: Reflecting and Problem Solving around Emotional Needs and Behaviour'. *Educational Psychology in Practice*. 11 (2) pp. 8–14.

Page, J. & Elfer, P. (2013) 'The Emotional Complexity of Attachment Interactions in Nursery'. *European Early Childhood Education Research Journal*. 21 (4) pp. 553–567.

Reddy, B. (1994) *Intervention Skills: Process Consultation for Small Groups and Teams*. Oxford: Pfeiffer and Company.

Schein, E. H. (1978) 'Career Dynamics: Matching Individual and Organizational Needs'. In: Turner, S., Robbins, H. & Doran, C. (1996) 'Developing a Model of Consultancy Practice'. *Educational Psychology in Practice*. 12 (2) pp. 86-93.

Schein, H. E. (1987) *Process Consultation: Its Role in Organization Development*. 2nd edn. vol. 1. Workingham: Addison-Wesley.

Schon, D. A. (1983) *The Reflective Practitioner: How Professionals Think in Action*. London: Temple Smith.

Stockley, S. (2003) 'Circles of Adults: An Exploration of an Experiential Process to Develop Teachers' Emotional and Professional Competency'. In: Wilson, D. &

Newton, C. (eds) (2006) *Circles of Adults: A Team Approach to Problem Solving around Challenging Behaviour and Emotional Needs.* S1. pp. 53. Nottingham: Inclusive Solutions UK Ltd.

Tickell, C. (2011) The Early Years: Foundations for Life, Health and Learning: An Independent Report on the Early Years Foundation Stage to Her Majesty's Government.

Vygotsky, L. S. (1978) *Mind and Society: The Development of Higher Mental Processes.* Cambridge, MA: Harvard University Press.

Wilson, D. & Newton, C. (2006) *Circles of Adults: A Team Approach to Problem Solving around Challenging Behaviour and Emotional Needs.* S.l: Nottingham: Inclusive Solutions UK Ltd.

Zuckerman, G. (2007) 'Child-Adult Interaction that Creates a Zone of Proximal Development'. *Journal of Russian and Eastern European Psychology.* 45 (3) pp. 43–69.

Work Group Supervision in practice
Developing pedagogy, self-understanding and teamwork

This chapter draws on four specific case studies which illustrate the impact of attending Work Group Supervision and the desire and motivation of the participants to challenge themselves as they begin to enjoy their work. This chapter uses the participants' own words to convey how the Work Group Supervision attended to the learning and development needs of all of the group members, encouraging individuals to get over personal difficulties and provide support for one another. This chapter takes the reader through each stage of the process, revealing growth and advancement in knowledge and self-understanding.

Working from a Vygotskyian perspective on group collaboration and peer learning, I have undertaken sustained work in recent years on the effect of Work Group Supervision sessions which explore the observation, assessment and planning practice of a team of Early Years educators. Denise, Kate, Julie and Erica attended ten facilitated group discussions over ten months, addressing specific observational issues to gain insight into how their key child was learning. These sessions gave the women an opportunity to engage in professional dialogue and robustly analyse their observations. This chapter outlines how pedagogy plays out in practice using Work Group Supervision as an intervention, addressing each stage of the process in order to focus on improvement.

The stages of the Work Group Supervision are (1) An individual presents their observation to the group and the focus is on that observation, (2) Discussion relating to the observation, with learning starting in a social context, (3) Reflection on how information from that observation might be used in unpicking meaning in a process of internalisation, and (4) Action and decision making – the facilitator guides the group's learning via focused questions and positive interactions.

What are pedagogical skills? And how do these manifest themselves in the Early Years educators' practice? Siraj-Blatchford et al. (2002:10) define pedagogy as:

> the instructional techniques and strategies that allow learning to take place. It refers to the interactive process between teacher/practitioner and learner and it is also applied to include the provision of some aspects of the learning environment (including the concrete learning environment, and the actions of the family and community).

These "instructional techniques and strategies" involve being able to use observations of children at play to aid effective holistic teaching, and learning that builds on previous learning. It requires Early Years educators to understand that children learn through their first-hand experiences, play and talk, and to support these they will need to be provided with purposeful and meaningful learning experiences. Pedagogy is more than professional knowledge and being well-qualified. Pedagogy and pedagogical skills and practice are influenced by a variety of factors, such as one's cultural beliefs and social background, as well as personal and political beliefs felt about children.

Moyles, Adams and Musgrove (2002:1) note:

> Early Years' pedagogy is an extremely complex phenomenon comprising a wide variety of practices underpinned by principles acquired through training and as a result of professional experiences and personal understandings. Because of its complexity, 'effectiveness' has to be viewed as a whole rather than as particular aspects taken in isolation.

The Early Years educators' expectations and ability to interpret and implement curriculum areas of learning are included in the pedagogical whole. Observational documentation serves as an important part of this. This includes the Early Years educators' ability to notice, recognise, respond appropriately, record observations, analyse, question and reflect on them, and engage in discussion with colleagues. It is clear that pedagogy develops from a range of factors that guide one's practice. In this way pedagogy informs both the curriculum and Early Years educators' interactions with children, in the experiences they offer and how they organise the learning environment inside and outside to help with appropriate development and learning. It reflects and supports the principles of observations articulated in Chapter 1.

Work Group Supervision in practice

Stage 1: Part 1

This stage provides time for educators to reflect on what they have observed children doing. Educators' observations are crucial to informing their practice. These observations of children's play are used to facilitate discussions about – stages of development – the child's interests – the ideas that they might be incubating – schemas or developing skills. These recorded observations are central to Work Group Supervision because they reveal not only what educators are noticing but also whether they recognise how children are developing. This first stage is designed to reveal what knowledge adults bring to their observations and how open-minded they are about the children. This requires one member to present a particular observation to the group and interpret what they think is happening.

Case study examples of two observations presented for discussion can be seen here:

Malcolm, aged 24 months

Fred was in the home corner with two other children. One child was putting wooden pizza pieces together and then cutting them apart with a toy knife, handing a piece of pizza to Malcolm. Malcolm would play at eating the piece of pizza before giving it back to the child, making a sound to cut it again. The child and Malcolm did this over and over again.

Malcolm banged the bricks together, then built a tower and knocked it down. He spent time knocking the bricks together and looking around him. He then stood the yellow brick up and knocked it down with his head. He did it again, and when the adult laughed, he did it a second time, watching for a reaction. He then banged the bricks again and looked around the room.

Owen, aged 30 months

Owen was sitting on the floor by a black tray containing train pieces and track. He started to pick out pieces of track and put them together one at a time. Owen was totally focused on what he was doing, not distracted by any of the other children playing around him. Owen then connected the pieces of train together to make a longer one and sat for a long time moving the train around the track. The only time Owen was distracted was when a child knocked his train off the track. Owen calmly said, "Hey that's my train", and placed it back to where it was. A couple of minutes later the same child came back and took the train again. Owen said calmly, "I had it first", and the child gave it back. Owen continued to play for a little while longer, then, when he had finished, he placed the trains and track back in the tray.

> *The next day I put the trains and track on the black tray out again on the floor. Owen returned to this activity, where he repeated his actions from the previous day, connecting all the pieces of train together to make a longer one. He then moved it around the floor and around himself making choo-choo noises. Choosing some bridge pieces, he joined them together and moved the train up and down, over and under the bridge, still making the choo-choo sound. He was totally engaged in what he was doing and was not distracted by any of the other children playing around him. Again, when he had finished, he put all the pieces back in the tray.*

In our first example Kate presents an observation on the experience of talking about her work to the group. This is challenging for her as Kate feels shy and lacking in confidence – the prospect of speaking to others in a group is probably quite frightening. But when she reflects on the beliefs that she has held about herself she becomes aware that they limited her understanding and she decides to reject them. The Work Group Supervision has helped her to accept and understand how her own perceived inadequacies may have affected her perception of her ability to communicate effectively – this increased her confidence. The process can be a challenge as Kate explains:

> It is a confidence thing for me. It was quite daunting at first to [present], but once you get into talking about it, it's not as hard as you think. Besides, the knowledge other people have given me, and the feedback I've got, it's helped me lots. Standing up in front of people talking, even though they are my close colleagues, it's still a bit daunting – have I produced good enough work, if you like. It's that sense of achievement that I have done it – I can do it. I am just like everybody else really, it is just that I am shy.

The emphasis of self and the increase in confidence is apparent. The participant sees the additional knowledge this will bring as being a central element in emphasising her sense of self. She is making a choice to understand her perceived inadequacies. Seeing herself as working with others is a significant construct in her self-understanding. The fear of being seen as incompetent had led to her placing limits on her capabilities. It is evident that, after the group supervision, she still has a fear of talking in front of the group. However, it is greatly reduced. The analysis shows that the group supervision has helped Kate to work through her fears and develop communication skills in ways that go beyond her own perception. Work Group Supervision can therefore provide staff with encouragement, acknowledge their strengths and weaknesses, and contribute to their ongoing professional development. The process can also help to develop a more trusting relationship, where participating adults can see that the focus is not on looking at their weaknesses but trying to develop their observational practice.

In the following account, Denise also highlights how the Work Group Supervision has helped her to challenge and change herself. Once she knows which child is being discussed, she can picture them, question others openly, and get answers. Recalling details vividly with others becomes central to her practice, so Denise's sense is that she feels "better prepared" to deal with the challenges, if and when they arise. In the two quotes below, she describes how she starts to "wise up".

> It prompted my memory, made me think what I had seen. You can see it, you know? You can visualise it, especially as it was the week before. I think it helped, especially if you were going to ask questions, because you are going to be discussing something that has happened a while ago.

> So, it makes me feel better prepared – once I'm asked questions about that particular child, I can visualise what's being discussed because I've just refreshed my memory. I like the way you read the observation and then you leave it open, and say 'What do you think?' Most of us know we have to wise up and think about the reasons our children might be doing things.

Stage 1: Part 2

This stage is designed to uncover what misconceptions and barriers may exist about children learning through play. This involves the participants working in pairs and reflecting on their pedagogical response to the observation being discussed. In the following account, Denise realises that she has been jumping to conclusions, adversely affecting her understanding. She begins to use observations to identify the facts about children's play and starts to think more deeply about the evidence. In this extract, Denise describes how she begins to notice play between children and how she contemplates supporting it.

> My presentation to the group made me realise that he needed more. I mean the child he was playing with was really helpful and really kind and it made him want to go back and play with him, because he was so gentle with him. I encouraged the other child to say words to him and it made me realise that he needed... modelling, and that maybe I should do that.

The Work Group Supervision has given Denise an opportunity to be more aware of her own thinking. Most importantly, it has changed her understanding of herself regarding what the child needs from her and she begins to realise that the support provided before the Work Group Supervision was not enough. Through discussing observations in the group, participants start to appreciate how communication may vary.

Stage 2

The second stage is intended to mediate learning through interaction with more knowledgeable others. This requires participants to work together in small groups of four. In the extract below, Julie describes how she begins to solve her problems in collaborative ways. This leads to her reflecting on and challenging her assumptions as she finds new ways of thinking. Encouragingly, the evidence suggests a shift away from her own assumptions to those which empower her to develop her understanding and find solutions. This suggests that the Work Group Supervision is critical for Early Years educators in this process.

> I was concerned about Laura, my gut feeling was that it wasn't autism.... I'd worked with two boys previously – they all asked me, and I said: 'I don't think so, but I don't know why she's flapping. I know, let's have a discussion with Stella'. And I was really relieved, to be honest. The girls had brought it forward and I knew it was going to be a challenging discussion, and I knew as a group we would all put our input in. And really, between us, we did find the answer. And we did it like two of us together, then two of us again, or two over here, but I think one of the big lessons is, girls, don't do it individually, do it as a group. You find out so much more, because we're all working in the same room and each one of us is missing something out.

The analysis finds that sharing perspectives is an important factor in bringing the group together and allows Early Years educators to share their ideas and enable thinking – this leads to an increase in skills and knowledge gained directly from each other.

Stage 3

Stage 3 highlights the importance of using observation as a tool to question why and how children do particular things in their activities. This requires all the group members to be open to learning in becoming an observer. Here, Denise discusses talking to her colleagues about child development and learning, how her interactions make her more aware of the child's thinking, and the context of their particular interests. Moreover, Denise appreciates the extent to which a considerable part of her work as an Early Years educator involves talking to her colleagues, observing the child, and thinking about how to support and extend their learning. The Work Group Supervision has allowed Denise to gain understanding about what the child knows and can do and her approach to learning. It has also helped her to recognise the children's progress.

> Just to look at the child and the whole aspect of it, talking about what we have seen, how we are going to move them on, and with everybody's input, it just opens up all these ideas – 'Ooh, we can do this', and 'Ooh, we can do that'. It just makes it more exciting. We can move it on and put new challenges in for them. I find it very helpful.

Work Group Supervision can be a collaborative effort that provides an opportunity for empowerment to meet individual and group responsibilities. Kate's account shows her growing confidence in her capacity to work together with others while learning about the children. It also illustrates her engagement and willingness to listen to the reflections of others.

> Everyone just comes together really, and they are quite respectful of your opinions and when you are talking, they listen. We are all in the same room in the setting most of the time together, and we are always saying 'I have seen that' or 'He was doing this and she was doing that'.

Stage 4

The purpose of the last stage is to provide the Early Years educators with pedagogical knowledge and understanding. This requires them to observe, interpret and discuss their observations of children learning through play and together find ways to support and scaffold this learning.

In the following account, Erica makes the case for continuing the facilitated Work Group Supervision, while also pointing to the usefulness of the structure. She conveys quite clearly that the Work Group Supervision has helped all of the staff to reflect on their understanding and allowed them to think more deeply.

> I think the evaluation at the end was very helpful... useful with reasons why a child might be doing a certain action, or their characters, and it made us all think, 'Oh! That is why they are doing that'. It has really, really helped all of us since this project's been going on.

The structure of the supervision is designed to empower the group in three ways – giving the adults time and freedom to behave according to their understanding;

empowering the adults to make decisions about their work; and encouraging accountability and trust. Julie says:

> I think it has benefited me because I think all my children will develop differently, now I observe them differently. I think I am helping them more. In a way, I feel like it has given me a boost to help them with new challenges.

Work Group Supervision plays an important role in ensuring that adults who work with babies and young children are provided with a regular space to learn about the things that they do each day. Consider how adults interpret and understand what they see. How open-minded are they? Are observations based on what is really happening or what the adult supposes to be happening? It is very important that adults see what is really happening in children's play. If adults have a narrow mindset, they may not have a holistic picture. The main aim of Work Group Supervision is to provide adults with time and space to talk about their observational work, as a way to ensure that they understand what they see. Any concerns adults have about their observational practice are addressed within the group session. Supporting job performance and the emotional engagement of each presenting adult, by making their observational work more open and accountable, helps them to learn from mistakes. Work Group Supervision can support adults to be more effective, helping them to think more deeply about what they see happening in play and the quality of the learning environment and their interactions.

It is interesting to note that nearly all of the participants in my study reported that they had felt empowered by the process and acknowledged the structure of the discussion as the guiding force. Work Group Supervision not only provides professional training and development, it also empowers adults to resolve issues over presenting, while feeling trusted to do so. If facilitated well, the group dynamic ensures that the participants feel that they are being listened to. Opportunities are created to interact with colleagues, get involved in discussions, ask questions and be actively involved in the problem-solving process. Implicitly, time spent sharing observations with colleagues encourages both individual and group accountability.

Work Group Supervision provides opportunities for adults to:

- Discuss issues relating to child development and emotional well-being – particularly concerning what is already known about the child, including the child's prior learning and what they know and can do
- Notice where significant learning is taking place and identify how best to support and extend learning
- Consider the effectiveness of their approach
- Receive support to improve personal effectiveness and professional practice

Developing pedagogy and self-understanding

To understand the value of the Work Group Supervision, one needs to examine how the Early Years educators interacted as a group, whether as part of their individual presentation, or working in pairs or as part of a smaller group. Concurrently, the conclusions reached by many researchers are that group discussion is more effective than one-to-one supervision – other researchers have found evidence that facilitated group discussion is a better option. Elfer and Dearnley (2007) determine that group supervision allows for increased interaction, resulting in the Early Years educator feeling listened to and supported. Manning-Morton (2006) finds that the Early Years educators' increased interaction leads to a growth in professional self-confidence with respect to working together and articulating their practice.

The Early Years educators participating in the Work Group Supervision expressed a clear preference for finding things out together, rather than on their own. The data yielded by this study provides convincing evidence that the group supervision offered the Early Years educators a critical view of their practice. The involvement of others is crucial in shaping not only their self-understanding but also the nature of their interactions with each other.

Denise: Relationships with a key person

The account below demonstrates how the presentation exposes Denise's strengths, weaknesses and gaps in her knowledge and in doing so creates an opportunity for her to think much more critically about her interactions with children.

> I think the attachment on my side was, 'I am not doing any good. What am I going to do?', where really I should have looked at the positive side. The positive side was that he was happy. He was contented, and he was just a little bit frustrated. And the minute I saw that he was getting frustrated because he could not talk, someone said 'You know, Dee, you should use sign language'. The advice that was given there... you look at the positive side of things, not the negative... they probably didn't even realise at the time how they were helping me. I mean, everybody knew I was upset at the presentation, as I was crying. But I think it was to realise other people feel the same thing as me and we're all in this together. He's your key worker child and you feel the responsibility, you have to do his paperwork, but, hey, you know we know that too. You see what I mean? I think that one of the things that's happened in the group sessions with you is that we've become more of a team. We always were a team, but I think the discussion side of it, especially the younger ones, they are not afraid to say what they think. They know, that they are not going to be judged by others on what they say.

Hanko (1999) finds that collaboration leads to high levels of interaction between group members and this can result in better outcomes for children. Similarly, Bain and Barnett (1986), Hopkins (1988), Elfer and Dearnley (2007) and Elfer (2012) show that Early Years educators become more aware of children's individual needs as a result of their interaction in the group. Hanko identifies the collaborative process as an important factor that allows Early Years educators to better their knowledge and skills. Work Group Supervision is just as successful as one-to-one supervision if facilitated well. The facilitator will need to know when to provide guidance to group members in order to support their collaboration through each stage of the process. This also means attending to the emotional needs of the group. Schein (1987) emphasises that the facilitator is key to developing the group's learning through supporting them to work together as they move through each stage. He also finds (1987) that work group discussions can be transformative, as the Early Years educators are involved in meaningful discussions; this creates opportunities for them to deeply reflect on their practice and their emotional responses to infants and young children. In this sense, learning occurs when individual Early Years educators generate, obtain and share knowledge and information. Change occurs as a direct result of their interactions with the group through each process. This allows them to move away from working on their observations alone towards group interactions and shared learning.

It is clear from Denise's response that the change in her self-understanding occurs very quickly after the Work Group Supervision and she is very aware of it taking place. More importantly, Denise reports gaining a better understanding of herself and being less negative in her interactions with the child. Denise identifies and builds on her understanding and this helps her to gain confidence, feel less like a failure, reduces her sense of isolation and encourages her to take control of her relationship with the child. Bain and Barnett (1986) speak of Early Years educators becoming more responsive to the children, while Hopkins (1988), Elfer and Dearnley (2007) and Elfer (2012) report Early Years educators making more thoughtful observations. The Work Group Supervision has given Denise an opportunity to hear different opinions about the same observation without judgement, which has contributed to her feeling that they are now a team. It has also given Denise the opportunity to reflect on their work.

Kate: Knowing and communicating

This next account highlights the benefits for Kate of hearing multiple perspectives about her child, as well as understanding more about play. It also relates to how she starts to allow open communication to take place with her colleagues. Kate explains that, before the Work Group Supervision, she had held back from interacting with others because she was shy. Reflecting on how she communicated with them, she becomes more aware of how much she has learned from others. This leads Kate to ask herself important questions about her perceived fears of talking to the group. The Work Group Supervision allows Kate to release her doubts and concerns and to open herself up. It also helps her to feel more confident, to speak up, and learn. It is clear that the more Kate applies the perspective of others to her work, the more understanding she gains about the child, which leads to an increase in confidence. It is interesting to note that once Kate presents her work to the group and experiences their positive reaction to her insights, she is more able to engage with them.

In the following extract, Kate describes her anxieties and how she overcomes her reluctance to interact with others:

> Before, I was quite shy, and I would feel that I wasn't being heard – but that's my insecurities coming out I suppose. Now I am open to talk about it, come out and say, 'Look this is what I think'. My opinions do count. I am not worried about going to them now and asking questions. Before, I wouldn't, I would just sit back. And they go, right, OK, and they advise me on how I go about it. It's a confidence thing for me and it helped me in that way.

Work Group Supervision requires each group member to participate in different interactions. At this level, it is necessary for the person presenting to communicate their assumptions to the group, such as their interpretation of what is happening. In addition, relationships within a group must be built and maintained because they are composed of individuals with different personal and professional knowledge bases and abilities. The role of the facilitator here is to determine the best guidance for supporting individuals to speak publicly in the group. The chosen strategy should enhance learning about working with different personalities.

Motivation is a key factor in group supervision, where Early Years educators present their observations based on their level of understanding. According to Wilson and Newton (2006), participants begin to feel less self-conscious speaking about their work. Therefore, the structure of the group processes for sharing ideas on what they know about child development and learning and how to support progression is important. Also, the pairing and smaller group processes can help shy participants feel more comfortable (Louis, 2017).

Work Group Supervision is an important approach for supporting the development of professional knowledge, which can then be immediately applied to one's practice. Schein (1987) reiterates the benefits of group work, which promotes individual accountability and encourages motivation and collaboration. In addition, Bain and Barnett (1986) say that work group discussion is one of the most effective ways to support Early Years educators to improve their day-to-day practice. If the participants are motivated and open to listening to the ideas of others, this may indicate that the process is going well.

The structure of the Work Group Supervision creates a set of processes that are interdependent of each other, starting with the first stage, where the presenter's observation is influenced by the reaction and interaction of the group. It is this essential aspect that makes group members so highly likely to participate. Ultimately, the process allows the participants to promote and support each of their individual achievements, improve effectiveness and use appropriate individual and collaborative skills (Wilson & Newton, 2006).

Erica: Observing and responding

In the next account Erica tells how the Work Group Supervision provides her with a space to focus her observations and challenges her to stand back, examine in detail what the child is doing, and consider her own response. In this extract, she describes the benefits of her new method of observing:

> I was so different – it's given me a clearer insight of what I can see and what I can do with them. Actually, just observing them, not having to have a pen and paper there. Watching what they are doing, it has benefited me.

Later, Erica reflects on how she has deepened her knowledge of child development. She realises that the Work Group Supervision has been pivotal in helping her to re-evaluate her practice. Her recollections particularly emphasise how she engages in the process of learning from her observations and the impact this has had on her practice and perspective. It is interesting to note that her views on many aspects of her work contrast markedly with her perspective before the Work Group Supervision. For Erica, to be able to explain her practice to others is highly significant to her understanding about herself. Here she illustrates the impact of this change of perception on her practice:

> It has helped with my talking, with my staff – it has helped me better my observations. I have noticed my observations have come on leaps and bounds from doing the course. It's actually helped me with activities, just to support them. Like today, I did the creative table, normal watercolours, and then I thought: 'No, I'm not going to stop there, I'm going to do something else.' And I got all the play dough and all the cups out with the children. I was like, 'Come on then.' The temp lady was saying, 'Oh, do we have to do this.' I said, 'No, just let them do it.' I was just standing back, even though normally I'd be like: 'No.' I'd be pretty hands-on with them, but I just stood there, saying, 'OK, fill that cup up for me'. We were asking open-ended questions and we had discussions about what they were doing. It was amazing and that is how I could see that I have

changed a lot, because before I'd be like, 'No! You have to use the cup properly and do this...'

What clearly emerges from Erica's account is the way in which she feels she has developed self-awareness. She discusses feeling motivated by the Work Group Supervision and how it has transformed her observational practice and increased her confidence. Erica clearly makes links between her observation tasks, development needs, interests and thinking beyond outcomes. She seems to have a new-found excitement about her role and feels that she knows the children and herself much better. Erica clearly recognises that sharing and reflecting as a team has brought about more cohesion and respect for each other. The assertion of self in standing up to her fears is indicated by her willingness to gain insight from others and also be less possessive about knowing her key children.

The quality of interaction in the group determines how the supervision facilitates learning and creates a positive group dynamic. Work Group Supervision can encourage individuals not only to articulate their practice, but also to locate themselves in it through speaking about it. Motivation and levels of engagement will be high if Early Years educators are able to interact and engage with others to achieve a shared goal and understanding throughout every stage of the process. Providing Early Years educators with a framework of support is critical to the development of their professional knowledge, leading to enhanced confidence and becoming more attuned to child development and learning. If we wish to see confident Early Years educators who are able to articulate how children are progressing, and how they plan to support each child to develop and learn, then we have to offer Early Years educators a structure which can provide the required levels of support, such as a collaborative work group where they can engage confidently with pedagogy and practice.

Julie: Learning together

During the Work Group Supervision, Julie's understanding of child development begins to increase. She starts to better understand aspects of her work. Interestingly, as this happens, her perception towards herself changes. Julie explicitly points to how the group discussion helps her to integrate her understanding into her work. In this extract, she describes how she becomes interested in the group sharing their viewpoints and opinions about the child:

> I think our discussions have helped all of us. When we are in the room, we all talk as a group about a child and we all have a little input. It kind of links us all together.

While Work Group Supervision aims at facilitating a group of peers to work together and gain better understanding, it also aids their overall professional knowledge and development. It is clear that it contributes to the participants' interaction, understanding and collaboration with other members of the group. Equally clear is the increase in the participants' personal and group responsibility. Work Group Supervision allows Julie to share her knowledge and, at the same time, maintain the diversity of the group's ideas. This account shows that Work Group Supervision can be more successful when the group members develop self-understanding among themselves; when they respectfully listen to the opinion of others; when members make concessions about their individual opinions for the sake of another; and when they engage actively towards reaching a shared understanding and goal. Julie describes a process in which everyone in the group is encouraged to contribute and where discussion and critical reflection takes place.

> I think that in helping some of the other girls here, I've grown in confidence. If they ask me something, I may be able to give them a better explanation for certain things if they want help with their children.

Julie recalls how she supports a colleague by providing the right level of relevant knowledge and experience to navigate their way through new assessment reporting systems and points to the degree in which her confidence increases by communicating her ideas and helping others. It is likely that the Work Group Supervision has helped Julie utilise her knowledge and skills because it has given her a platform to express her understanding, which increased her confidence. It has also helped her to use her understanding of the colleague's perspective to inform the level of support that she provides.

> Earlier on, a colleague was having a review and she asked me about this two-year progress check, to go through with the parents what it actually was. I just said that it's a kind of assessment of where their child's at and what stage they are at, but that's fine within their age range and not to worry about it. She was a bit worried about it, so I just helped see her through that and she was OK.

The link between growth in professional confidence and collaboration is established in Schein (1987) and Hanko (1999). Manning-Morton (2018) notes that a lack of confidence may compromise how Early Years educators interact with team members and help infants and young children to develop and learn. In his study, Farouk (2004:208) finds confidence amongst teachers increases, particularly "where personal feelings may have come to intrude into their professional practice". He further notes that the group context acts as a resource for the Early Years educator to share knowledge and understanding and behave as an adviser, helping others in the group to become aware of a range of factors which may impact on the situation under discussion. This ability to support one's colleagues, so that they can clearly see how children are progressing, involves recognising another person's gaps in knowledge and supporting them to develop and master new skills. Hanko notes that work groups which focus on specific gaps in knowledge are central to formulating collaborative learning and the growth of self-confidence. She supports the view that structured discussion is important and points out that teachers' confidence seems to be a key factor underpinning the extent of their effectiveness and ability to engage with children.

Learning together as a team

According to Vygotsky (1978), such understanding is constructed initially on a social plane before it can be internalised and developed as the learners engage in social and cultural activities.

An important part of the Work Group Supervision is having an opportunity to discuss observations with others in depth – this can help adults to focus on what is significant and what they notice, while providing insight into what others notice. One way to start addressing the challenges discussed earlier is to facilitate Work Group Supervision sessions that will bring to the fore insight about existing knowledge and skills, and attitudes on child development and the observational process. The value of the Work Group Supervision is that it is designed to provide additional support and guidance specifically on observational practice. There are opportunities throughout for the participants to pause and reflect on their practice and to invite other group members to consider whether there is scope for any improvement. Work Group Supervision is also a tool to assess and evaluate observational practice and processes. My research suggests that group supervision may be a predictor of effective observational practice. It has a direct impact on the quality of observations because the process focuses on everyday observational practice. Here, Erica describes how she begins to solve her problems in collaborative ways. This leads to her reflecting on and challenging her assumptions as she finds new ways of thinking.

> Being able to come together with everyone and exchange information and ideas about the same children we are all working with really helps us to think more deeply about them and the reasons behind why they do some of what they do – they are not just being naughty.

Hamachek (1999:209) believes that a teacher's personal knowledge and understanding of themselves is fundamental to their practice. He poignantly states: "Consciously we teach what we know; unconsciously we teach who we are." In other words, the beliefs and values that teachers hold in relation to teaching, learning and self-reflection are an important component of professional growth. Similarly, Murphy et al. (2007) claim that it is necessary to bring implicit beliefs about teaching and learning forward to render them explicit. The participants' accounts suggest that sharing perspectives is an important factor in bringing the group together. The data indicates that it allows the Early Years educators to share their ideas and enables thinking, increasing the skills and knowledge they gain directly from each other. Encouragingly, the evidence suggests a shift away from their own assumptions to ones which empower them to develop their understanding and find solutions, suggesting that the Work Group Supervision is critical for Early Years educators in this process.

Here, Kate's account reveals how she begins to shift her perspective and take up those of others when she makes decisions about planning and next steps in learning.

> If [my colleagues] see things that I have not, they tell me, 'Did you know that he can do this?' And we talk about it. I am often given information that I have not noticed before and I use it to plan for the next steps, to take him on to the next level, the next step of learning. It's helped me a lot. The group was coming up with different sensory explorations and stuff and that was interesting, to get that feedback from them – you look at things in a different light. It's very interesting – other people's opinions and the knowledge that comes out of them.

This account demonstrates that Kate considers advice from others to be valid enough to follow. This leads to her looking at the issues from a much broader viewpoint while learning from her colleagues. In the same vein, the next extract shows an appreciation of collaborative learning. Erica admits to realising that her fears started out as being a barrier to her progress but goes on to describe how the variety of insights within the group cause her to consider different views and feel less defensive.

> I used to get really frustrated. I used to be like, 'You don't know my key children', a little bit defensive, 'That's not what they're doing, how can you tell?' Now, I'm like, 'No, bring it on. Let me know what you know'.

Ultimately Erica has become less possessive about her key children and demonstrates a greater sense of cohesion and respect towards her colleagues. Erica's fear of being judged is exposed during the group supervision but this has a positive influence on how she becomes more open to the idea of learning from others. In relation to showing support, the analysis reveals increased confidence in communicating ideas. Next, Erica highlights how supportive the process is and that she has gained a deeper understanding of her work – her confidence increasing as she begins to communicate her ideas more effectively.

> I think that by helping some of the other girls here, I've grown in confidence. If they ask me something, I may be able to give them a better explanation for certain things if they want help with their children.

The evidence suggests that, because of the group supervision, Erica is more supportive of her colleagues and this has an impact on her confidence. Between them, the participants seem to be developing a sense that they should provide support and guidance to others – with the most experienced and knowledgeable modelling this for their colleagues.

During the Work Group Supervision, Denise's understanding of child development begins to increase, and she starts to better understand aspects of her work. Interestingly, as this happens, her perception towards herself changes. She explicitly expresses how the group discussion has helped her to integrate her understanding into her work. In this extract, she describes how she becomes interested in the group sharing their viewpoints and opinions about a child:

> I think our discussions have helped all of us. When we are in the room, we all talk as a group about a child. We all have a little input and it links us all together if that makes sense.

These participant accounts make a strong case for Work Group Supervision which supports Early Years educators to examine the practices that undermine their confidence, while encouraging them to develop their knowledge, skills and understanding. In participating in the group supervision, what is unfamiliar challenges their thinking. The Early Years educators are then able to move their personal and professional understanding about children's learning to a new level. In addition, the removal of the developmental descriptor as the only reference point challenges their beliefs and encourages reflection through group discussion, promoting changes in their understanding about children and themselves. These significant changes, recorded in the interviews and focus group, provide further evidence that they become more reflective about how they meditate on their practice. The study finds variations across all four women – from one who recognises her attitude as a factor and acknowledges her own lack of understanding, to others who deepen their understanding about children and the conditions that facilitate learning. The findings indicate that the Work Group Supervision has helped to expand their perception about themselves and children's learning, while enabling them to take responsibility for their practice.

Notably, all the participants who took part in the Work Group Supervision reported a growth in self-confidence. The group supervision is intended to address all the challenges faced by Early Years educators in respect of observation work, helping to ensure personal and professional growth of knowledge and understanding in every facet of the process – noticing, recognising, deciding and interacting. It provides them with a set of tools enabling them to foster the most supportive way of working with their colleagues, with a focus on learning from meaningful experiences that are essential for building up the professional confidence of others.

Conclusion

To conclude, understanding what drives and shapes the Early Years educator's practice is important. Participation in the Work Group Supervision can enhance self-awareness; improve professional practice and development; and thereby provide insight into how knowledge and skills impact on play, talk, engagement with others, infants and young children. However, lack of self-understanding on the part of the Early Years educator may lead to them withdrawing from a child or responding inappropriately, impacting on children's emotional well-being. While it is acknowledged that Denise, Kate, Julie and Erica have some of the knowledge and skills required to do their job. It is critical that we consider how their knowledge and skills are translated into their everyday practice.

In the next chapter we focus on the observer and the decisions that they make.

Bibliography

Bain, A. & Barnett, L. (1986) 'The Design of a Day Care System in a Nursery Setting for Children under Five'. *Document No. 2T347*. London, Tavistock Institute of Human Relations [TIHR].

Brown, A. & Bourne, I. (1996) *The Social Work Supervisor: Supervision in Community, Day-Care, and Residential Settings*. Buckingham, UK, Philadelphia, PA: Open University Press.

Elfer, P. (2012) 'Emotion in Nursery Work: Work Discussion as a Model of Critical Professional Reflection'. *Early Years: An International Research Journal*. 32 (2) pp. 129–141.

Elfer, P. & Dearnley, K. (2007) 'Nurseries and Emotional Well-being: Evaluating an Emotionally Containing Model of Professional Development'. *Early Years*. 27 (3) pp. 267–278.

Farouk, S. (2004) 'Group Work in Schools: A Process Consultation Approach'. *Educational Psychology in Practice Theory, Research and Practice in Educational Psychology*. 20 (3) pp. 207–220.

Hamachek, D. (1999) 'What They Do, How They Do It, and the Importance of Self-knowledge'. In: Lipka, R. & Brinthaupt, T. (eds.) *The Role of Self in Teacher Development*. pp. 189–224. Albany, NY: State University of New York Press.

Hanko, G. (1985) *Special Needs in Ordinary Classrooms: From Staff Support to Staff Development*. 3rd edn. London: David Fulton.

Hanko, G. (1999) *Increasing Competence through Collaborative Problem Solving: Using Insight into Social and Emotional Factors in Children's Learning*. London: D. Fulton Publishers.

Hawkins, P. & Shohet, R. (2012) *Supervision in the Helping Professions*. 4th edn. Maidenhead: McGraw-Hill, Open University Press.

Hopkins, J. (1988) 'Facilitating the Development of Intimacy between Nurses and Infants in Day Nurseries'. *Early Child Development and Care*. 33 (1) pp. 99–111.

Inskipp, F. & Proctor, B. (1993) *The Art, Craft & Task of Counselling Supervision Part 1: Making the Most of Supervision*. Twickenham: Cascade Publications.

Inskipp, F. & Proctor, B. (2001) *Becoming a Supervisor*. London: Cascade.

Kadushin, A. (1992) 'What's Wrong, What's Right with Social Work Supervision?'. *The Clinical Supervisor*. 10 (1) pp. 3–19.

Kelchtermans, G. (2009) 'Who I Am in How I Teach Is the Message: Self-Understanding, Vulnerability and Reflection'. *Teacher and Teaching: Theory and Practice*. 15 (2) pp. 257–272.

Kertzmann, J. P. & McKnight, J. L. (1993) *Building Communities from inside Out: A Path Towards Finding and Mobilising Community Assets*. Evanston, IL: Institute for Policy Research.

Louis, S. (2017). 'Examining the Impact of a Discussion Group on the Self-perception of Early Years Practitioners'. Unpublished.

Manning-Morton, J. (2006) 'The Personal Is Professional: Professionalism and the Birth to Threes Practitioner'. *Contemporary Issues in Early Childhood*. 7 (1) pp. 42–52.

Manning-Morton, J. (2018) 'Noticing, Recognising, Responding and Reflecting: The Process of Observing Infants and Young Children'. *Early Education*. 85 pp. 11–13.

Moyles, J., Adams, S., & Musgrove, A. (2002) *SPEEL: Study of Pedagogical Effectiveness in Early Learning*. London: Department for Education and Skills. Research Report 363.

Murphy, C., Beggs, J., Carlisle, K. & Greenwood, J. (2007) 'Students As 'Catalyst' in the Classroom. The Impact of Co-Teaching Between Science Student Teachers and Primary Classroom Teachers on Children's Enjoyment and Learning of Science'. *International Journal of Science Education*. 26 (8), pp. 1023–1035.

Proctor, B. (1997) 'Contracting in Supervision'. In: Sills, C. (ed) *Contracts in Counselling*. pp. 190–206. London: Sage.

Proctor, B. (2008) *Group Supervision: A Guide to Creative Practice*. London: Sage.

Rustin, M. & Bradley, J. (2008) *Work Discussions: Learning from Reflective Practice in Work with Children and Families*. The Tavistock Clinic Series. London: Karnac Books.

Scaife, J. & Scaife, J. (2003) 'Supervision and Learning'. In: J. Scaife (ed) *Supervision in the Mental Health Professional: A Practitioner's Guide*. pp. 15–29. Hove: Routledge.

Schein, H. E. (1987) *Process Consultation: Its Role in Organization Development*. 2nd edn. vol. 1. Workingham: Addison-Wesley.

Siraj-Blatchford, I., Sylva, K., Muttock, S., Gilden, R., & Bell, D. (2002) *Researching Effective Pedagogy in the Early Years*. London: Department for Education and Skills.

Soni, A. (2013) 'Group Supervision: Supporting Practitioners in Their Work with Children and Families in Children's Centres'. *Early Years: An International Research Journal*. 33 (2) pp. 146–160.

Steel, L. (2001) 'Staff Support through Supervision'. *Emotional and Behavioural Difficulties*. 6 (2) pp. 91–101.

Stringer, E. T. (1996) *Action Research: A Handbook for Practitioners*. London: Sage.

Stringer, P., Stow, L., Hibbert, K., Powell, J., & Louw, E. (1992) 'Establishing Staff Consultation Groups in Schools'. *Educational Psychology in Practice: Theory, Research and Practice in Educational Psychology*. 8 (2) pp. 87–96.

Vygotsky, L. S. (1978) *Mind and Society: The Development of Higher Mental Processes*. Cambridge, MA: Harvard University Press.

Wilson, D. & Newton, C. (2006) *Circles of Adults: A Team Approach to Problem Solving around Challenging Behaviour and Emotional Needs*. S.l: Nottingham: Inclusive Solutions UK Ltd.

Zuckerman, G. (2007) 'Child-Adult Interaction that Creates a Zone of Proximal Development'. *Journal of Russian and Eastern European Psychology*. 45 (3) pp. 43–69.

Using observation to tune into children – and its challenges

This chapter examines the key role of observation and latent tensions and challenges in the process of observing. It will provide further insight into how Work Group Supervision can support teams of Early Years educators to closely observe the detail of what happens and why children do what they do, showing the clear links between the group supervision and improvement in pedagogy and practice.

Many theorists and educators, such as Friedrich Froebel (1782–1852), Susan Isaacs (1885–1949), Lev Vygotsky (1896–1934), Jean Piaget (1896–1980), Chris Athey (1924–2011) and Tina Bruce have encouraged us to look more closely at the play children initiate for themselves and to learn from them. Adult observations are important – not only are they the foundation of their understanding about children's explorations and learning, they are a vital tool in getting to know individual children. Once Early Years educators know how to observe, they are better able to track children's progress – identifying issues of concern becomes an integral part of the process.

Froebel in Lilley (1967:79) recognises the challenges of observation when he says:

> Observation of children is just as important for us too. In doing so we catch sight of our own far-off childhood, which, like our own faces, we can only see in the mirror. Through our observations we come to understand ourselves and our own life, that they become for us an unbroken whole.

Froebel's profound insight begins with his assertion that children are unique and different. He reminds us that adults sometimes superimpose their own recollections, understandings and aspirations onto children. This is not necessarily a bad thing. As Froebel says, it is a way of making sense of our own lives, as well as trying to get to grips with understanding children, while Bruce (2019, personal correspondence) states: "Our childhood mingles with our adult life and the two together form an unbroken whole."

The most striking evidence from the Work Group Supervision concerns the changes found in the observational practice of Early Years educators. The study reveals many significant improvements consistent with the findings of Papatheodorou (2009). These include increasing knowledge, skills and understanding about the process of learning, instead of only observing the content. The Early Years educators appear to engage more with children that they previously struggled with. Furthermore, Early Years educators note improvements in the children's learning because of the Work Group Supervision.

In relation to the Early Years educators' own learning, they indicate that they have gained new knowledge and skills in observing children's development and learning, further confidence in observing learning through play and improved relationships with the children, at the same time re-evaluating the pedagogical process. It is therefore possible that the process of group work and collaboration allows Early Years educators to reflect on their observations on a more conscious level, making them more inclined to analyse them. The evidence suggests it cannot be supposed that Early Years educators know how to observe children.

The first challenge is deciding what to observe. The mere act of asking someone to observe assumes that they will know why and what to do. Even if we only focus on the question of *why* we observe, we find that understanding it is as crucial to the process as *what* we observe. Adults cannot observe children holistically or effectively if they do not first understand the reasons behind why they are observing them. How adults observe will influence and affect what they consider to be important. However, the crucial question is whether adults make accurate, detailed and conscious observations of what they see children doing – do they recognise progress and create further openings to support and deepen learning?

Why observe?

Here, Erica recalls how discussions with her colleagues have contributed to her learning more about herself and a child. She notes how "everyone could see clearly what he was doing" and she could not. Erica realises that the issues are her own. This realisation prompts reflection, which helps her to gain insight and better understanding of herself and her abilities. She becomes intrigued by the process of the discussion and decides to challenge her limiting beliefs about herself. Her account also illustrates how the experience has made her aware of the extent to which her views on the child had been influenced by her own insecurities:

> The first work group session that we did with trucks, I was, like, 'What's he doing? He is just sitting on a truck, pushing a truck around in a circle, round and round' When I looked at it, I didn't get it. Then, when we had the discussion, it

> was just interesting how everybody could see clearly what he was doing. I feel more confident now. I feel like I am working with children that I actually know. Before, I might have thought, 'I've not got a clue what that child is doing – I do not know why he is roaming around the trucks', but, actually, when you break it down in the discussion, I do know my children.

Brodie (2015:22) recognises that carrying out observations is essentially a moral practice aimed at being aware of our own views and looking at them through the lens of "children's rights", to make sure that every child is respected, included and supported. However, the extent to which current observational practice is matched to Brodie's notion of ethical observation has serious implications for developing observational skills to more effectively meet the developmental needs of children. Sadly, some Early Years educators see observations as a "chore" (Osgood, 2012: 127). This view is echoed by Wood and Attfield (2005:97), who propose that some Early Years educators may be more inclined to adopt a "watching and waiting" approach for development and learning that can be documented, in order to match it to the prescribed outcomes of a child's progress. They imply that such practices lack pedagogical interaction which can advance learning and development. Similarly, Drummond (2012:49) argues that some Early Years educators "look for what they expect to see, at the expense of picking up on the glimpses of unintentional learning that children may hint at in their play".

These kinds of observations are not good for children – they do not seek to notice the detail of what they are doing and saying, which is a vital part of understanding how to support learning. Neither are they good for pedagogy, because they do not allow Early Years educators to do the thinking necessary to make adjustments in their interactions or learning environment, to facilitate children's learning based on an understanding of their individual strengths, weaknesses and interests (Bruce, Louis & McCall, 2015). Due to the centrality of observations within Early Years educators' practice, it is important that there is further investigation into how best to support them to develop the skills to do this morally and ethically.

What to observe?

What educators observe will depend on several factors, such as their beliefs about development and learning, what information they would like to find out about the child, their knowledge and understanding about how children learn, their ability to implement and interpret the curriculum, and their relationship with children. Educators need to observe everything that they see and hear with infants and young children. This means observing their interests; the way they walk, talk and pretend; their facial expressions; the way they challenge themselves by persisting with difficulty;

how they communicate with others; how they take responsibility; schemas; and emerging learning. Some educators find the process difficult, which may be due to them being introduced to observations as a technical task. Here, Denise tells how she starts to pay more attention to the nature of play and learning in her observations:

> Now I know I will find something. In the old days [before the WGS] I used to just think, 'You [the child] are just sitting there doing nothing…I'm not watching them, what a waste of time…' Now, my whole outlook comes to the point where I think, 'Let's watch them.' Then I get my observations. So, in the end, I've got everything I need, that week, if I watch them.

Denise reveals that her lack of confidence had resulted in her only observing behaviours which she knew. It also indicates that her approach was affected when she was faced with a play or learning situation that she did not then confidently understand. The way that Denise used to observe may have led her to focus more on the content of the framework, rather than developing an understanding of the children.

Supporting development and learning

In the next example Julie presents an observation on how she started to observe everything that she saw and heard children doing and saying. Her new approach to observations seems to have helped her to learn a lot about her teaching and children's development and learning. This underlines the intention of Work Group Supervision as a vehicle for professional development and, in turn, supporting children's developing learning. Educator's observations are key to supporting development. As this next extract shows, Julie also notes changes in how she acts on her observations and uses this information to find out about the children's knowledge.

> I found out that I knew a lot more about the child that I observed than I thought I did. It has taken me to new levels of observing and knowing that child and looking deeper into what they are doing. Like Laura with the flapping – when I see it now, I try to think 'Why is she doing that, is she excited?' I observe her facial expression and maybe lead her into something that will keep her engaged throughout the day.

Julie recalls how she has begun to sharpen her focus, leading to "new levels of observing". She associates her improvement with the experience of the Work Group Supervision and regards it as a major turning point in becoming aware of previously unfamiliar aspects about the child's development. She also recognises that she is better at observations than she had thought, which suggests a new understanding of self is beginning to form. More importantly, she begins to probe and question herself. She considers how the child is learning and, as a result, finds herself adapting to their perspective, which ultimately increases her self-understanding. This suggests that, before the Work Group Supervision, Julie had underestimated the potential and ability of children, resulting in lower expectations, specifically when the children did not have spoken language. It also indicates that her lack of understanding about how children communicate may have influenced her understanding of the child's abilities. Afterwards, she can better understand the child's involvement signals, such as facial expressions, and provide appropriately for that child. Zuckerman (2007) suggests that the adult's, and child's, Zone of Proximal Development is affected when the adult knows that the child might need help. She argues that when adults focus on what is present in the child at the moment of meeting, connecting the fragments of the experience into knowledge of their self-identity, it leads to higher mental functions, as is presented in the extract above.

Making learning visible

In the following account, Erica comments that her observations start to encourage critical thinking and questioning of what she has seen. The evidence suggests that the Work Group Supervision has had an impact on her self-awareness – particularly its influence on the way in which she pays closer attention to her observations.

> I'm doing a lot more watching than I used to. When I'm watching now, I'm thinking, 'Why are they doing that? Or how could they do it differently?', instead of just watching them play. I feel like my brain is always ticking over, trying to help them.

Similarly, Erica's account shows an increase in confidence about her beliefs and knowledge of children after the Work Group Supervision. It is clear that her perceptions of learning are associated with her ability to make connections between play and learning. It is possible that her practice is influenced by other factors, such as her relationships with colleagues.

The evidence also suggests that participating in Work Group Supervision can close the gaps in the observational skills of Early Years educators – although it is difficult to prove conclusively that it has a direct impact on their observations. Increasing confidence in observing is key to improvements in practice and, in this study, the Early Years educators' confidence does increase. These findings strongly suggest that the group supervision may provide a way of combining the link between knowledge and practice through focusing on developing confidence in Early Years educators. Manning-Morton (2006), Elfer and Dearnley (2007) and Elfer (2012, 2014) identify ongoing Continuing Professional Development opportunities as being very important to supporting Early Years educators in a deeper understanding of the personal and emotional aspects of their work. All three authors suggest a change in the way professional development is delivered. They imply a move away from short one-day courses to ongoing group opportunities, which allow Early Years educators to develop self-awareness and to emotionally, personally and professionally engage with their practice.

It is important to note that the Early Years educators participating in the Work Group Supervision report that they started to move away from drawing conclusions based on one observation in isolation, to analysing shared observations as a group. They started to consider a range of factors, which included how their style of interaction may affect children's learning, rather than blaming children for not developing. The findings from this study provide evidence that Early Years educators enter the workforce with misconceptions about child development. Their perceptions then guide their practice. The Work Group Supervision offers opportunities for examining their assumptions about children and practice.

All the Early Years educators in this study report that the Work Group Supervision has enabled them to challenge their own understanding of themselves. They change their perceptions and attitudes, respond to others in different ways, and overcome self-doubt to become better at analysing and understanding their own reactions to children. These findings suggest that they also develop the confidence to question who they are as Early Years educators. Shifts in perception and understanding feature notably in the analysis.

The second challenge is writing up observations that make children's learning visible. This process is dependent on adults having knowledge of child development and being able to notice learning, interpret and listen carefully, then use that information to capture it in a short narrative. However, in many nurseries where adults have curriculum frameworks to follow, they may simply copy the developmental milestone as an observation. Clearly, knowing just what to write down is an important part of the process. How adults record their observations can reveal what they value and how their personal and professional experiences influence the way that they are interpreting, noticing and recording the children's learning.

How to write observations?

According to Manning-Morton (2006): "Adults begin to learn how to write observations when they understand what ideas children might be exploring and are able to notice significant learning." Generally, we use all sorts of words to describe the complexities and connections that we see in children's play. Finding the right word, and learning how to combine observation with a narrative, is trickier than one might think.

It is a skill that takes time to develop. It is important to keep in mind that there are many different ways to record significant learning. What is also important is that adults are supported to develop the art of writing a factual short story from their perspective. Behind the act of writing up, an observation is based on having a sound understanding of how children learn and knowing what significant learning looks like.

Educators who struggle with writing observations can improve their skills and techniques by participating in Work Group Supervision. The focused facilitated discussions are designed to help them understand and more easily recognise and support children's significant learning. The important process of scrutinising observational practice can lead to discussions about child development as well as opportunities to share what others have observed. In the following example, Kate points to how her confidence develops, so that she is more able to describe meaningful learning.

> I find now that I am writing more observations, whereas before I would struggle with them. I would write loads, then cross them out. Now I feel confident. We have been observing two of our key children a week and I have been adding my observations to the board. I held back before – now it has given me the confidence to write more observations.

This extract shows that, before the Work Group Supervision, Kate had a lack of observational skills in describing and recording how children were learning. It also indicates that she previously lacked confidence in her ability to master writing observations down and that she needed reassurance. It is apparent that her confidence to carry out observations was affected by several factors, including a lack of experience and a fear of getting it wrong in front of team members. This would suggest that the Work Group Supervision has helped her to establish and develop her observational practice. It also reveals that Kate previously felt frustration at the process of writing her observations because of her lack of skill as an observer. Before the group supervision she did not know how to write careful observations, nor did she know that the child might do things that were part of their learning – her lack of understanding had left her disempowered. Not only is it a personal triumph for Kate but it has also enhanced her observational skills. Most importantly, when Kate reflects upon the degree to which her observations have improved, she realises that her confidence and abilities as an observer are growing – the group supervision has deeply affected her understanding of her capabilities. There is a direct link between the process and the improvements in her practice, as well as the changing culture of the nursery as a result of participating. After the group supervision, Kate shows more willingness to write observations – not caring about mistakes but learning from them instead. An equally important aspect of Work Group Supervision is reaching a group decision about how much and how well the child has learned. This gives adults responsibility for developing learning and the children's environment, based on what they now know, as opposed to the learning outcomes set out in a framework.

Learning how to write child observations is a skill that takes time to develop and refine – it requires practice and years of experience to be done well. This means that educators must have a reasonable knowledge of child development, the curriculum, and the structure of play. It is vital that educators recognise and understand what significant learning looks like for infants and young children, so that they can make decisions concerning the child's development. Work Group Supervision facilitates meaningful conversations about observations – talking about and unpicking children's developing learning helps the educator to recognise and describe it.

The following criteria for writing observations is provided:

1. In what ways do children struggle with new experiences?
2. Do children explore a particular concept?
3. How do children manipulate and discover new things?
4. How do children practise their newly-acquired skills?
5. Recognition of schemas
6. What materials does the child play with?
7. What do they do with the materials?
8. What problems do they encounter and how do they solve them?
9. What are the child's interests?
10. What do they like to do?
11. What choices do they make?
12. Who do they play with?
13. What kind of play do they choose?
14. How do they communicate – verbally, non-verbally?
15. What do they say?
16. What kind of questions do they ask?
17. To what extent do they use language to describe events and tell stories?
18. What kind of experiences do they share?
19. Do they get involved in pretend play?
20. What do they represent symbolically in models, drawings and paintings?

Recognising significant development and learning

The process of observing babies and young children is both physical and emotional. Sometimes emotional feelings are hard to bear, particularly when children display difficult or challenging behaviour that we do not understand or know how to manage. The detrimental impact on children's development and learning as a result of adults not noticing, recognising, or appropriately responding to them in everyday situations is clear. This is why adults need both time and space to reflect on their observational practice. As Denise says:

> I realised that he is not doing it to be a pain, he's doing it for a reason. My attitude changed… not that I didn't want to be around him, it was just that I felt that I was failing him.

Reflective questions

- To what extent are your observations of children helping you to connect consciously to their play?
- Look at the observations you are gathering for individual children. Do these properly detail their first-hand experiences?
- Are children given appropriate times to play?
- Is play fluid in the setting or is it constantly being interrupted?
- Are you dedicated to gathering observations during play activities that children initiate for themselves?

Linking theory to practice

The third challenge is how adults apply their professional knowledge and experience. Personal values, beliefs, professional background and experience influence what is observed. Unless those adults who lack knowledge about how children develop and learn are provided with appropriate support and guidance, there is a danger that they either try to hide behind developmental checklists or observe only what they know at a superficial level, thus missing significant development and learning. More often than not, an adult's interpretations of observations do not include any reflection or discussion. As a result, they do not understand their significance. Here Denise describes how the Work Group Supervision has helped to facilitate conceptual change:

> I think I have always thought of schemas when I write observations. But I never thought to include it. Now, my whole outlook of writing observations is, 'Look, that's a schema', or 'How could I enable the children to do it more', or 'What are they doing?', not thinking, 'Oh, this child is really being a pain in the neck', but more, 'There must be a reason why they want to do that'.

Important themes emerge throughout the interview with Denise. Probably the most significant concern the improvement in her self-understanding about how young children play and the development of a more objective perspective. These help Denise to engage in her observations more effectively and her understanding starts to increase significantly. After the Work Group Supervision, she begins to monitor and manage her own emotional responses – she is less likely to become frustrated or rush to interrupt the child's play. It also gives her an understanding of how to work with young children, which reduces her worries about her lack of training.

In analysing Denise's position, there is a clear shift in her sense of self. This is reflected in how she begins to use the knowledge of theory to help her to look at the child in another way. Consequently, she starts to value their play differently. Denise's account indicates potentially important changes in self-understanding. Her focus shifts from feeling stuck to one where she becomes more aware of her choices. For example, Denise starts to perceive children differently – she stops underestimating them and begins to question some of her values. The group supervision provides her with the opportunity to develop the understanding she needs to progress, increasing her confidence and sense of self. Denise also becomes much more motivated in her work and more aware of her responses.

It is also clear that the Work Group Supervision enables Denise to develop self-understanding about being and becoming a better observer, while also helping her to articulate and clarify her values in practice. The ideas generated in the group supervision discussion empower participants to increase their awareness and appreciation of the children, developing their self-understanding by enabling them to interact with their own experience and the ideas of others. Consequently, they become more willing to be part of the group supervision and acutely aware of what they do not know. Increases in knowledge and skills are associated with collaborative learning. Thus, from a Vygotskyian perspective, Denise's understanding of schema theory can be seen as a dynamic process resulting from revealing her interpretations to others, thereby allowing herself to act more effectively.

It is noteworthy to mention that when Early Years educators have an understanding of the schematic theory of Jean Piaget and Inhelder (1969), further developed by Chris Athey (1990) and notable writers such as Tina Bruce (1991), Cathy Nutbrown (1999), Cath Arnold (1999, 2010), Stella Louis et al. (2008) and Tasmin Grimmer (2017), it may help adults to consider their role in relation to:

- Knowing why children do some things in certain ways
- Having an understanding of the importance of repetition and initiation
- Having a clear purpose for observing children
- Knowing about each child's interests and preoccupations
- Knowing how to introduce new language to describe the child's actions
- Knowing how to observe, support and extend learning
- Providing worthwhile learning experiences
- Providing open-ended resources and materials
- Having the ability to share knowledge of how children learn with their parents
- Seeing children as active learners

Conclusion

Finally, what the Early Years educators choose to do differently in their practice as a result of attending and participating in the Work Group Supervision conveyed a sense of their increased confidence and understanding. Crucially, skills in carrying out observations become more established, so that Early Years educators are better able to write, describe children's learning, analyse and interpret observations in light of new information gathered from others. We need to consider how best to support Early Years educators to develop knowledge of meaningful observational practice with infants and young children.

In the next chapter we examine the observer, their interactions and relationships with infants and young children.

Bibliography

Arnold, C. (1999) *Child Development and Learning 2–5 Years: Georgia's Story.* London: Paul Chapman.

Arnold, C. and the Pen Green Team (2010) *Understanding Schemas in Early Childhood.* London: Sage.

Athey, C. (1990) *Extending Thoughts in Young Children: A Parent-Teacher Partnership.* London: Paul Chapman.

Brodie, K. (2015) *Observation, Assessment and Planning in the Early Years: Bringing It All Together.* Maidenhead: Open University/McGraw Hill.

Bruce, T. (1991) *Time to Play in Early Childhood Education.* London: Hodder and Stoughton.

Bruce, T. (1997) 'Adults and Children Developing Play Together'. *Early Childhood.* 5 (1) pp. 89–99.

Bruce, T. (2001) *Learning through Play: Babies, Toddlers and the Foundation Years.* London: Hodder and Stoughton.

Bruce, T. (2019) 'Personal Correspondence.'

Bruce, T., Louis, S., & McCall, G. (2015) *Observing Young Children.* London: Sage Publications Ltd.

Drummond, M. J. (2012) *Assessing Children's Learning.* London: Routledge.

Elfer, P. (2012) 'Emotion in Nursery Work: Work Discussion as a Model of Critical Professional Reflection'. *Early Years: An International Research Journal.* 32 (2) pp. 129–141.

Elfer, P. (2014) 'Social Defences in Nurseries'. In: Armstrong, D. & Rustin, M. J. (eds) *Social Defences against Anxiety: Explorations in the Paradigm.* pp. 284–299. Tavistock Clinic Series. London: Karnac.

Elfer, P. & Dearnley, K. (2007) 'Nurseries and Emotional Well-being: Evaluating an Emotionally Containing Model of Professional Development'. *Early Years*. 27 (3) pp. 267–278.

Froebel, F. W. (1887) *The Education of Man*. New York: Appleton.

Grimmer, T. (2017) *Observing and Developing Schematic Behaviour in Young Children: A Practitioner's Guide*. London: Jessica Kingsley Publishers.

Hamachek, D. (1999) 'What They Do, How They Do It, and the Importance of Self-Knowledge'. In: Lipka, R. & Brinthaupt, T. (eds) *The Role of Self in Teacher Development*. pp. 189–224. Albany, NY: State University of New York Press.

Isaacs, S. (1930) *Intellectual Growth in Young Children*. New York: Harcourt.

Isaacs, S. (1933) *Social Development in Young Children*. New York: Harcourt.

Isaacs, S. (1968) *The Nursery Years*. London: Routledge and Kegan Paul.

Lilley, I. M. (1967) *Friedrich Froebel. A Selection from His Writing*. Cambridge: Cambrige University Press.

Louis, S., Beswick, C., Magraw, L., & Hayes, L. (2008) *Again! Again! Understanding Schemas in Young Children*. Lutterworth: Featherstone Education.

Louis, S., Beswick, C., Magraw, L., & Hayes, L. (2012) *Understanding Schemas in Young Children. Again! Again!* London: Bloomsbury.

Manning-Morton, J. (2006) 'The Personal Is Professional: Professionalism and the Birth to Threes Practitioner'. *Contemporary Issues in Early Childhood*. 7 (1) pp. 42–52.

Murphy, C., Beggs, J., Carlisle, K., & Greenwood, J. (2007) 'Students as "Catalyst" in the Classroom. The Impact of Co-Teaching between Science Student Teachers and Primary Classroom Teachers on Children's Enjoyment and Learning of Science'. *International Journal of Science Education*. 26 (8) pp. 1023–1035.

Nutbrown, C. (1999) *Threads of Thinking*. London: Paul Chapman.

Osgood, J. (2006) 'Deconstructing Professionalism in Early Childhood Education: Resisting the Regulatory Gaze'. *Contemporary Issues in Early Childhood Journal*. 7 (1) pp. 5–14.

Osgood, J. (2012) *Narratives from the Nursery: Negotiating Professional Identities in Early Childhood*. London: Routledge.

Papatheodorou, T. (2009) 'Exploring Relational Pedagogy'. In: Papatheodorou, T. & Moyles, J. (eds) *Learning Together in the Early Years*. pp. 3–17. London: Routledge.

Piaget, J. & Inhelder, B. (1969) *The Psychology of the Child*. London: Routledge & Kegan Paul.

Vygotsky, L. S. (1978) *Mind and Society: The Development of Higher Mental Processes*. Cambridge, MA: Harvard University Press.

Wood, E. & Attfield, J. (2005) *Play, Learning and the Early Childhood Curriculum*. 2nd edn. London: Paul Chapman.

Zuckerman, G. (2007) 'Child-Adult Interaction that Creates a Zone of Proximal Development'. *Journal of Russian and Eastern European Psychology*. 45 (3) pp. 43–69.

 Respectful interactions are everything

This chapter explores how Early Years educators interact with children, focusing on their emotional engagement, organisation of the learning environment and instructional support. With illuminating accounts, it also seeks to provide insight and guidance on how Work Group Supervision can be used to support Early Year educators to think more deeply about their teaching, interactions and responses with babies and young children.

We already know that what Early Years educators know about young children's learning is important; however, so too is the quality and nature of their interactions with them. According to Shore (1997) early interactions directly affect the way the brain is wired. Interactions are defined as the moments in which Early Years educators observe, interpret and teach, which includes all the things that adults do to help children to learn. An important aspect of educators' interactions is that they need to know that there are prime times for children acquiring different kinds of knowledge and skills. Speaking generally, it is not surprising that the question of interaction is never far from the surface when we think about observing or tuning into children. Like the question of observations, interaction confronts us in every aspect of our work with babies and young children. It cannot be avoided or ignored under any circumstances. However, it is equally important to recognise that the question of interaction has been treated rather superficially by many Early Years educators (Fisher, 2016). One possible reason is that they may believe that they should interact with children in order to "teach" skills and young children will learn when Early Years educators instruct them. On the contrary – children learn skills and understanding through meaningful play activities in which they have a purpose, as well as when Early Years educators understand how to guide and engage with children's learning. In this sense, Early Years educators' interactions are seen as teaching. Effective interaction therefore takes account of the children's interests, abilities, needs, relationships, learning and background. If Early Years educators start with observation, they can get to know children extremely well.

Getting to know children and building relationships with them

A good interaction is where Early Years educators are able to model language, explain how children might do something, facilitate a process, explain a concept and encourage children to think for themselves. In practice, Early Years educators are interacting with and responding to children all the time; however, how they interact relates to how they teach. It is this powerful interaction that will either value or disrespect children's play. When Early Years educators are not informed by their observations, they will not understand what level children are at or have knowledge of their abilities, confidence levels or what ideas they might be interested in pursuing. This can mean that they step in too soon, resulting in the child moving away. Moyles, Adams and Musgrove (2002:3) point out that a lack of self-consciousness on the part of the Early Years educator when engaging in discussions about their teaching may hinder support for children's learning and limit professional growth.

Clearly, lack of self-consciousness can alter the nature of an adult's interactions with children. It may hold back the very skill that they are trying to develop instead of moving learning on by standing back, observing, and drawing on what is known about the child. This is why it is so important to start with observation – if Early Years educators are observing and listening to children, they will know when the moment comes to support, guide or extend learning. Each interaction must take account of what is known about the children, while recognising that each child is different and will require different responses.

Respecting and appreciating children

Early Years educators will have continuous interactions with children throughout the day. In each one they should be observing, interpreting and teaching. The child will only make progress if they get this right. Unfortunately, too many Early Years educators don't have time to carefully consider their interactions or reflect on why they treat certain types of play negatively – this may have an impact on children's learning. In the account below, Denise makes it clear that she previously needed someone else to tell her about her interactions and interpretation. In her account, she reveals what she had been thinking about 2-year-olds at that point:

> I felt I was failing the little boy I was going to present. I needed encouragement. I had this big barrier in my head – 2-year olds, all they do is make a mess and you have to change nappies, and I thought of all the negative sides of it. I think I just needed somebody to say, 'Do you know what he has just done? Do you know what he is learning and how you could support them better?' The excitement in Stella made me think about what I saw. I call it my learning journey. It is like a journey of a discovery, the pair of us, me and this little boy…

Denise's response is particularly noteworthy because it suggests that the Work Group Supervision has given her permission to seek the support that she knew she needed to improve her practice. It is also clear that the group supervision has helped Denise to learn from the experience of others and become more compassionate towards the child. Moreover, her excitement at the Work Group Supervision enabling discussions, which showed what the child was doing well, appears to have helped her to see the child differently. Work Group Supervision discussions can help Early Years educators become more skilled at recognising learning, development and progress by encouraging them to think about how they are supporting children to direct their own learning. Work Group Supervision allows important time to examine their interactions with children from their observations and helps Early Years educators to reflect on how effectively they have observed, interpreted and responded to the experience. In fact, the process provides a specific focus on how their interactions take account of children's prior learning, abilities and interests while thinking about their interactions from the children's perspective.

Reflecting on the quality of interactions

Work Group Supervision also provides further opportunities for Early Years educators to reflect on whether they are engaging with children emotionally and equitably, while also considering why they respond to children and activities in a particular way. Ultimately, the process can help Early Years educators get to know their children much better and develop confidence and understanding when interacting with them. If facilitated well, Work Group Supervision has the potential to enhance the quality of interactions in Early Years settings; adults interfere less because they know their children. It is clear that the question of interaction forms an integral part of Work Group Supervision discussions. It is critical that Early Years educators understand the difference between supporting children and interfering in their play. Put simply, when adults support children in their play, development and learning, they have noticed what children do and are trying to do. Interfering in play comes when the Early Years educators see little or no value in what children have chosen to do by themselves. Instead, they push through their own "teaching" agenda, which may be meaningless to the children, resulting in them losing interest.

Knowing when to intervene

One of the most difficult challenges that Early Years educators face is knowing when to intervene and when to step back. Bayley (2008) states that observations are central to the way in which adults offer, develop and extend play opportunities for children. This is also in line with Buldu (2010), who says that adults need to be knowledgeable and confident if they are to sensitively intervene to help the child to learn and progress. Yet, the view of interactions held by adults is undoubtedly linked to how they teach and how they draw on a range of teaching strategies to take children to the edge of their capacities.

Early Years educators' relationships with children are important and central to children's learning, suggesting that they are involved in a social relationship with children, colleagues and parents. This is where Vygotsky's concept of the Zone of Proximal Development is pertinent, particularly as Early Years educators are required through their observations to identify the moment when children need support. Vygotsky's constructivist perspective on learning considers the connection between cognitive development and affective factors in learning and problem solving. Hopkins' research recognises that work discussion groups can support Early Years educators to deal with the complexities of relationships in which they find themselves, particularly those who work with children under the age of 3. Similarly, Elfer and Dearnley (2007) say that taking part in work discussions raises awareness of the emotional demands of Early Years practice. Elfer (2012) asserts that taking part in work discussions can reduce feelings of loneliness and the pressure to remain positive towards the emotional demands of the job. In the following extracts, Denise describes changes in her self-understanding and interactions:

> I have realised that whatever they do is for a reason. You know? It is not that they are being naughty, like the other day the two 2-year-olds were at the brick table. Malcolm building a tower was quite good in what he was doing. Well, these boys just went 'Boooom!' Every brick was on the floor. I walked in and Claire said – she was showing this lady around – 'Denise, what do you think?' And I said, 'Ooh, who was that? What lovely 2-year-old did that?' The mum laughed, and I said, 'Ooh, you both had fun, mmmmm'. The mum said, 'But it's all on the floor'. And I replied, 'That's what they need to do'. Claire said, 'You have changed'. [Laughs].

> I used to hate it when the children poured the sand in together and then mixed everything, I love sensory play. I love mess. But this used to really irritate me, you know. They put the sand in the water. Now it is like, 'Oh they have to do it, let them do it'. And when someone goes 'They are doing this…' I say, leave them.

Important themes emerge throughout Denise's account. Probably the most important concern the development of her self-understanding, how young children play, and a more informed and purposeful perspective. These help Denise to participate with her observations more effectively and her understanding starts to increase significantly. After the Work Group Supervision, Denise begins to monitor and manage her own emotional responses – she is less likely to become frustrated or rush to interrupt the child's play. It also gives Denise an understanding of how to work with young children, which reduces her worries about lack of training. Further analysis of Denise's account demonstrates that there is a clear shift in her sense of self. This is reflected in how she begins to use knowledge gained from the Work Group Supervision to help her look at the child in another way. Consequently, Denise starts to value their play differently. She now feels a new sense of joy and pride in her work and discusses it without feeling overwhelmed, because it now has new meaning.

Clearly, if we believe that knowing when to interact, to intervene, to provide appropriate support or give the right answers to children is important, then so too must be the idea of supporting Early Years educators to be more respectful and engaging in their interactions with children.

What kind of support is appropriate?

Early Years educators need to talk with children about what they say and do and what interests them – and they must listen carefully to how children respond. This is essential, because through such conversations children not only learn new words and practise using language, but they may also tell you something about how they feel, their ideas and their relationships. Most importantly, by talking with children about their play, Early Years educators are showing that they are interested in what they do and that it is important to them. It is therefore fundamental that Early Years educators tune in to what children are telling them through their play and responses.

Although talking to children about their interests is important, sometimes Early Years educators do not know what to say. They may say something quite general that has nothing to do with what the children are doing. Communicating and interacting with children using open-ended questions may be new to many Early Years educators. If this is the case, they will need to practise this kind of questioning. When they learn how to do it, they will feel comfortable in using this method of engaging and interacting with young children. Here, Kate describes how she has moved away from intervening, how she has started to observe and now waits to be invited into the child:

> Don't intervene – let them take their play to a new level, not spoil it by going, 'Oh, what colour? How many?' but at the same time learning from them. If you intervene too early, they'll just get up and leave and disperse somewhere else. They sometimes bring you into their play – bring you into their little world, whatever their activity is, and they're asking you questions, instead of me going, 'What are you doing?' or 'What are you not doing?' It's about them trusting you and letting you come into their play.

Throughout Kate's account, there are consistent themes around the perceived advantages of not intervening in the children's play. When she reflects upon the extent to which she had previously tried to lead and structure it, she becomes aware that the children were not engaging; instead, they were abandoning their play. Kate realises that this was a consequence of her interference and she now resists the temptation to ask inappropriate questions while they play. This clearly shows that the Work Group Supervision has influenced Kate's perception and the decisions she makes about the kind of interactions she is going to have with the children in her care. Following the group discussions, Kate changes her approach. Instead of intervening, she begins to observe, which suggests a change in her understanding about valuing play and supporting learning. It is most likely that the Work Group Supervision has helped Kate to understand how to support children's play and her role in assisting and extending it, which increases her confidence in her ability to do her job more effectively.

Using observations to connect with children

In the next example, Denise seems to be searching for meaning from her observations in her attempt to further develop herself. Denise particularly highlights that her observations are "deeper and more obscure", which suggests that the Work Group Supervision has been effective in helping her to think more objectively and change her behaviour – which also helps to reduce anxiety about her lack of training. Denise describes how she becomes considerably more supportive of the children's thinking in their self-initiated play:

> As I watch any of the children now, I don't go, 'Oh, this child is being a pain in the neck'. I watch, and I wait, and I've got the iPad, and I take pictures. Then I carry on watching and I take more pictures. I find now that my observations are deeper and more obscure, sometimes ones that you would not have got if

you did not wait and see it. You can be like, 'Oh look, they are playing with the castle', and you just sit there and ask them questions about what they are doing and the conversations that we have are unbelievable.

What clearly emerges is the way that Denise starts to see little things that would have gone unnoticed before the Work Group Supervision. Certainly, what Early Years educators say to children will depend on how the children communicate, what they do, what their interests are and what is known about their abilities. Describing children's play and interests and asking open-ended questions encourages them to continue to play. What is very important about asking open questions is that Early Years educators need to observe carefully and listen to how the children respond. When Early Years educators build on what children say and do, they help the play to be sustained.

Knowing when to interact and help

It is generally agreed that the quality and nature of interactions between Early Years educators and children contributes to learning and development. The Effective Provision of Pre-school Education (EPPE) Project, carried out in the UK from 1997–2004, studied the impact of early childhood education and care on development for children aged 3–7 years old. It involved 3,000 children who were recruited at age 3-plus and studied longitudinally over the life of the project. One of the study's aims was to pinpoint and characterise the most effective pedagogical strategies applied in Early Years practice to support the development of young children's skills, knowledge and attitudes and ensure a positive start at school. EPPE found that effective pedagogical strategies include Early Years educators having warm, interactive relationships with children, viewing educational and social development as complementary and equal in importance, and supporting children in making better all-round progress.

Effective interaction

Effective pedagogy includes interaction traditionally associated with the term "teaching", the provision of instructive learning environments, and "sustained shared thinking" (where a child and adult engage with the understanding of the other and learning is achieved through a process of reflexive co-construction). Practice which puts particular emphasis on literacy, maths, science/environment and children's diversity (catering to children of different genders, cultural backgrounds and abilities or interests) promotes better outcomes for children in their subsequent academic attainment (Sylva et al., 2004).

The EPPE research makes it hard to deny the impact of adult interactions on all play, development and learning. This observation taken from a nursery setting in London captures the quality and nature of the interactions with a group of three children.

> Sarah (4 years) spends 20 minutes in the sandpit outside, digging a hole and pouring water into it with a small plastic watering can, patting the sand when it becomes soggy and sprinkling dry sand on top. She then leaves and pushes a doll across the garden in a pushchair, goes to the block play area indoors, and watches some children constructing there. She stays only briefly and then moves on to the paint area. Here she pauses, takes a potty pan, and puts a spoon of yellow paint in it from a large tin in the middle of the table. There are five large tins of paint – red, blue, yellow, black and white. She scoops water from a jug in the middle of the table to mix the paint. She uses the different sections in the potty pan to make different colours, red, yellow and green, then she paints a person. James (2 years) arrives at the painting table. He begins to shovel paint, spilling as he goes, into a potty pan. The adult greets him warmly. 'Hello James, do you want to do a painting, or would you prefer to make mixtures? Look over there, you could make mixtures at the mixture table. Shall I show you?' He goes with her, and happily mixes gravel, sand and clay into sludgy bits in a potty pan. Mary (3 and a half years) joins Sarah. She watches and the adult asks, 'Would you like a potty pan? Take one from the shelf if you do'. Mary does this. 'Now just take one spoonful of the colour you like!' Mary does this. 'Now add one scoop of water and mix it with your spoon'. Quite soon Mary has made green out of yellow and blue and her intense concentration suggests that she is finding this very interesting to do.

An analysis of the adults' interactions shows that:

- Sarah, James and Mary are being offered what they need now
- Sarah is allowed autonomy to make choices and decisions and to use her skills and techniques to mix her own paints
- James is not ready to mix paints for himself and will just waste expensive resources if he is allowed to ladle paint everywhere and splash water onto it – but he is ready to learn how sand, clay and gravel behave when in contact with water. This way he can learn about the properties of materials
- Mary is ready to mix paints, but she needs a great deal of adult support as she is in the early stages of learning how to do it
- The adult nurtures each of the children's ideas, feelings, relationships, physical development and embodiment

- The adult does not crowd Sarah with too much attention when she needs personal space
- The adult respects James's needs, diverting him into something appropriate for him without making him feel bad about using the paints inappropriately, because he can't yet understand
- Mary is given help sensitively in a way which will build her confidence, skills and autonomy
- All the children are self-motivated because they are encouraged to be so. Their motivation to learn is not crushed, but nurtured
- Each of the children is developing self-discipline. This helps them to concentrate well and to learn effectively
- Because they are given choices, allowed to make decisions and given sensitive help as and when it is needed, Sarah, James and Mary are able to learn in ways which are right for each of them as individuals. The adult is supporting and also extending their learning
- Adults are emphasising what the children can do, rather than what they can't do. The tone and atmosphere are encouraging and not judgemental or critical. This builds self-esteem and confidence
- The adult knows that Sarah needs the personal space to mix the paint colours and then symbolically represent a person in her painting. The person is her mum. In this way she can develop as a symbol user
- James benefits from lots of talking with the adult about what he is doing and going to do
- Mary also needs lots of support in mixing paint and getting its texture right. Language, talking and listening to each other is an important and central way in which children become symbol users

Most importantly, whilst it might look as if adults are only there in the background, they are central. Adults working with young children, either in group settings or in a home-based setting, are key to helping children to develop and learn. Adults can create warm affectionate atmospheres which open children up to learning and help them to know themselves, respect themselves, like themselves, and engage with their learning positively.

Adult interaction and pedagogy

Bruce (1997:91–92) brings the delicate boundaries between unstructured and guided play to the fore. She presents it as "a rich vein of research on play", warning that this must not become a device for children to be "moulded into the shape adults and cultures desire, by using mechanisms such as 'guided play' or 'structured play'."

Generously, she acknowledges that mastering the correct balance when adults and children are playing together is quite a delicate exercise. She argues that the notion of adults developing, engaging and interacting in meaningful play requires the adult to "observe, support and extend play" (1997:97). In many Early Years settings there is sometimes a tendency for adults to take over the activities and experiences that they provide for children, as they may not yet have mastered the delicate balancing act as described by Bruce (1997). Stephen (2010) conducted a study about the types of pedagogy necessary for Early Years educators to support children in their understanding of technological toys at nursery and at home. She finds that they accept observation and interactions as being at the centre of their practice. However, asked about pedagogy, she notes that the issue "still disturbs some practitioners who find it more difficult to articulate how they act to support learning". On this basis, she states that they need more encouragement to think about the theories that underpin the practice of learning and teaching. In doing so, she raises a concern that there is a lack of "explicit engagement with pedagogy", and that this has become an intrinsic feature in Early Years practice, as it currently stands.

There is plenty of research evidence which suggests that the most powerful learning happens when children are allowed to lead, with the adult guiding them. However, there are times during the day, such as story time, when the interactions might be adult-led. Stewart (2011), in her study on the characteristics of effective learning, finds that some Early Years educators may take adult-directed activities to mean structured play, thereby limiting creative and learning opportunities for children. The Early Years educators taking part in the Work Group Supervision had mistaken the term "adult-led activities" to mean that they should take control to ensure that the children met their learning objectives. Indeed, two of the Early Years educators had taken the expression "hands-on" to mean an adult-led activity, where an adult would effectively manage a child's learning. The ways in which this can affect the quality of interactions with children are obvious – children's initiatives and ideas are unintentionally stifled and they quickly lose interest. Perhaps then it is unsurprising that Early Years educators repeatedly describe not knowing what kind of questions to ask children or how to help them move forward. It implies that outcomes may become more important than relationships and the process of children's learning, as is seen in the approach taken by the Early Years educators in this study.

Involving children in their learning

In the account below, Kate describes how she starts to involve the children in planning after asking them questions about their ideas. This results in her being less "hands-on" (adult-directed) and more able to follow the children's lead. It is evident that the Work Group Supervision has inspired her to provide a range of activities based mainly on the children's interests, rather than her own. After the group discussions, Kate has become more emotionally connected and able to take responsibility for planning activities within the nursery. This establishes an important link between her interactions in relation to her emotional engagement and awareness of the children's perspectives. Here Kate tells how she begins to respond more flexibly to the children's interests and motivations:

> I am planning for activities more now, involving myself a lot more in creative activities. I like to do creative activities, involving and asking the children their plans for what they would like, or what they would do, so it is going with the children, not just adult-led all the time. For instance, we had a box of shredded paper and the children just wanted to throw it at each other, so that is what we did. We had a great time just throwing it at it each other and it was lovely. They were laughing, joking, and running around with paper everywhere. So, yeah, it is going with them – going with what they want to play.

Kate's response is noteworthy because it suggests that she has a clear sense of purpose in her interactions and that she values the knowledge which the others contribute. It seems that the group supervision has helped Kate to operate from a position of confidence – she begins to behave very differently and provides an example of how she has become more engaged in her work. Kate indicates that increasing personal involvement in the planning process allows her to look for new ways to develop her skills and learn new ones. She starts to reveal aspects of herself to others and talks about her interest more. It is clear that the group supervision has helped Kate to become more aware of her thoughts and behaviour. It has challenged her to do her job more effectively, while reflecting upon herself and seeking out meaningful opportunities to further develop her understanding, resulting in more balanced interactions.

Tuning into children

In the next extract, it seems clear that the Work Group Supervision offers Erica an opportunity to develop and refine her interaction skills. She explains how she has stopped intervening by stepping back, reflecting, and thinking more about how the child is learning. Erica indicates that she feels more confident about asking for help. Moreover, she comes to understand what helps to facilitate learning for the child and describes here how she becomes more receptive:

> What do we get from watching them? Just so much – like how they take a simple sticking activity, they just drizzle the glue, and we are all like, 'You have got to

put stuff on that.' But no, actually, they don't. The process and the effect of what they are doing is drizzling that glue. I'm not going to stop them from doing it, whereas, as I said before, I would have said, 'Cover that glue up, you are going to get it all over the table.' But it's just changed a lot now, I can just sit back and watch, I am not going to ask what they are doing. It's made me much more of a nursery practitioner. My job is more worthwhile.

It is interesting to note that, before the Work Group Supervision, the participants had reported that they struggled during observations to understand how and when they should interact with the children. After the group supervision, the participants become more engaged with pedagogy and better able to improve their emotional engagement. In the next chapter, Erica sums up the prevailing view when she says: "I'm not interfering in their play." Key changes in their interactions emerge from the data. They start to use the information from their observations to inform interactions and planning. They feel more professional and engaged and they resist the constraints of the developmental descriptors. In reflecting on the group supervision, all the Early Years educators detail important shifts in practice, which they associate with their increased pedagogical understanding. The findings suggest that, before the group supervision, the Early Years educators engaged with their work on a surface level; afterwards they become significantly more emotionally engaged. These findings are consistent with the study by Manning-Morton (2006), which finds that changes in interactions are strongly associated with shifts in emotional engagement. This is also in line with Elfer (2014), who finds that Early Years educators become more thoughtful in their interactions.

Involvement scales, well-being scales and observing deep-level learning

Involvement and well-being scales are based on the work of Ferre Laevers (1997) in Belgium, who is interested in how children engage with "deep-level learning". Involvement scales indicate a child's level of contentment with what they are doing. These can help the Early Years educators build an understanding of the child's involvement levels, which can be rated on a scale from 1–5. Where the child is placed on the scale is not a decision about that child – it may indicate a lack of appropriate support or provision from the Early Years educator. It should also be noted that a child cannot be expected to function at Level 5 all the time, this would be exhausting! One factor that stands out with both the involvement and well-being scales is that when children are playing, they are emotionally engaged and physically active. When children are engaged in deep learning, they are busy doing things and experimenting in order to find out for themselves, for example, making a ball of clay into different shapes (a cupcake, a snake, small pieces, and then back into a ball again). Laevers describes how having the right learning environment can help children reach this special state of "involvement".

Signals include:

- Concentration – deep or easily distracted
- Energy – the way the child is talking and moving, including facial expressions
- Complexity and creativity – personal touch, on the edge of the child's capability or great enthusiasm
- Facial expressions and posture – alert body
- Persistence – prepared to put in effort to prolong the experience, asking for things to support play
- Precision – paying attention to detail
- Reaction time – very alert and focused or short-lived
- Verbal expression – language and the way of using it
- Satisfaction – immersed in an experience

Involvement scale level 1: Extremely low

Activity is simple, repetitive and passive. The child seems absent and displays no energy. They may stare into space or look around to see what others are doing.

Involvement scale level 2: Low

Frequently interrupted activity. The child will be engaged in the activity for some of the time they are observed, but there will be moments of non-activity when they will stare into space or be distracted by what is going on around them.

Involvement scale level 3: Moderate

Mainly continuous activity. The child is busy with the activity but at a fairly routine level and there are few signs of real involvement. They make some progress with what they are doing but don't show much energy and concentration and can be easily distracted.

Involvement scale level 4: High

Continuous activity with intense moments. At all times they seem involved and they are not easily distracted.

Involvement scale level 5: Extremely high

The child shows continuous and intense activity, revealing the greatest involvement. They are concentrated, creative, energetic and persistent throughout nearly all the observed period.

Laevers refers to involvement and well-being as the process variables that tell us how children are doing. He states that by "well-being" we mean "feeling at home" or "being oneself" – in other words, feeling comfortable in one's own skin. When observing well-being signals be particularly mindful of the four different types of attachment – see Chapter 11.

Well-being signals include:

- Openness and receptivity – the child seems to be comfortable
- Flexibility – adapting to changes in the environment
- Self-confidence and self-esteem – is able to explore the environment
- Being able to defend oneself – assertiveness, ability to express self, wants and needs
- Vitality – full of movement and energetic
- Relaxation and inner peace
- Enjoyment without restraints – when children are busy doing things, such as building with blocks, pouring and filling containers, playing in a puddle or moulding clay, sand or play dough
- Being and feeling comfortable in themselves

Well-being scale level 1: Extremely low

The child clearly shows signs of discomfort such as crying or screaming. They may look dejected, sad, frightened or angry. The child does not respond to the environment, avoids contact and is withdrawn. The child may behave aggressively, hurting him/herself or others.

Well-being scale level 2: Low

Posture, facial expression and actions indicate that the child does not feel at ease. However, the signals are less explicit than in Level 1 or the sense of discomfort is not expressed the whole time.

Well-being scale level 3: Moderate

The child has a neutral posture. Facial expression and posture show little or no emotion. There are no signs indicating sadness or pleasure, comfort or discomfort.

Well-being scale level 4: High

The child shows obvious signs of satisfaction (as listed in Level 5). However, these signals are not constantly present with the same intensity.

Well-being scale level 5: Extremely high

The child looks happy and cheerful, smiles, or cries out with pleasure. They may be lively and full of energy. Actions can be spontaneous and expressive. The child may talk to him/herself, play with sounds, hum, or sing. The child appears relaxed and does not show any signs of stress or tension. He/she is open and accessible to the environment and expresses self-confidence and self-assurance.

Conclusion

Lastly, sensitive and responsive Early Years educators have the ability, skill, knowledge and motivation to ensure that infants and young children's developing needs, learning and relationships are met. When Early Years educators take time to observe, listen and genuinely engage with infants and young children they inevitably tune into them as they play and learn, making it easier for them to know when to appropriately intervene. Being aware of what involvement and well-being signals and scales looks like in practice can help the Early Years educator to recognise and avoid periods of stress, and low emotional well-being and involvement for the child. We need to consider how we can use these indicators to gauge children's interests, well-being and levels of involvement.

In the final chapter we consider how to support developing professional practice.

Bibliography

Bayley, R. (2008) *Like Bees, Not Butterflies. Child-initiated Learning in the Early Years*. Lutterworth: Featherstone Education.

Brown, A. & Bourne, I. (1996) *The Social Work Supervisor: Supervision in Community, Day-Care, and Residential Settings*. Buckingham, UK, Philadelphia, PA: Open University Press.

Bruce, T. (1997) 'Adults and Children Developing Play Together'. *Early Childhood*. 5 (1) pp. 89–99.

Buldu, M. (2010) 'Making Learning Visible in Kindergarten Classrooms: Pedagogical Documentation as a Formative Assessment Technique'. *Teaching and Teacher Education*. 26 (7) pp. 1439–1449.

Elfer, P. (2012) 'Emotion in Nursery Work: Work Discussion as a Model of Critical Professional Reflection'. *Early Years: An International Research Journal.* 32 (2) pp. 129–141.

Elfer, P. (2014) 'Social Defences in Nurseries'. In: Armstrong, D. & Rustin, M. J. (eds) *Social Defences against Anxiety: Explorations in the Paradigm.* pp. 116–299. Tavistock Clinic Series. London: Karnac.

Elfer, P. & Dearnley, K. (2007) 'Nurseries and Emotional Well-being: Evaluating an Emotionally Containing Model of Professional Development'. *Early Years.* 27 (3) pp. 267–278.

Fisher, J. (2016) *Interacting or Interfering? Improving Interactions in the Early Years.* Maidenhead: Open University Press.

Hawkins, P. & Shohet, R. (2012) *Supervision in the Helping Professions.* 4th edn. Maidenhead: McGraw-Hill, Open University Press.

Hopkins, J. (1988) 'Facilitating the Development of Intimacy between Nurses and Infants in Day Nurseries'. *Early Child Development and Care.* 33 (1) pp. 99–111.

Inskipp, F. & Proctor, B. (1993) *The Art, Craft & Task of Counselling Supervision Part 1: Making the Most of Supervision.* Twickenham: Cascade Publications.

Inskipp, F. & Proctor, B. (2001) *Becoming a Supervisor.* London: Cascade.

Laevers, F. (1994) *The Leuven Involvement Scale for Young Children. Manual and Video.* Leuven, Belgium: Centre for Experiential Education. Experiential Education Series No 1.

Laevers, F. (1997) *A Process-Oriented Child Follow-up System for Young Children.* Centre for Experiential Education: Leuven University, Belgium.

Laevers, F. & Moons, J. (1997) *Enhancing Well-Being and Involvement in Children. An Introduction in the Ten Action Points.* [videotape]. Leuven, Belgium: Centre for Experiential Education.

Manning-Morton, J. (2006) 'The Personal Is Professional: Professionalism and the Birth to Threes Practitioner'. *Contemporary Issues in Early Childhood.* 7 (1) pp. 42–52.

Moyles, J., Adams, S., & Musgrove, A. (2002) *Study of Pedagogical Effectiveness in Early Learning.* London: DfES.

Proctor, B. (1997) 'Contracting in Supervision'. In: Sills, C. (ed) *Contracts in Counselling.* pp. 190–206. London: Sage.

Proctor, B. (2008) *Group Supervision: A Guide to Creative Practice.* London: Sage.

Rustin, M. & Bradley, J. (2008) *Work Discussions: Learning from Reflective Practice in Work with Children and Families.* The Tavistock Clinic Series. London: Karnac Books.

Scaife, J. & Scaife, J. (2003) 'Supervision and Learning'. In: J. Scaife (ed) *Supervision in the Mental Health Professional: A Practitioner's Guide.* pp. 15–29. Hove: Routledge.

Shore, R. (1997) *Rethinking the Brain.* New York: Families & Work.

Soni, A. (2013) 'Group Supervision: Supporting Practitioners in Their Work with Children and Families in Children's Centres'. *Early Years: An International Research Journal.* 33 (2) pp. 146–160.

Steel, L. (2001) 'Staff Support through Supervision'. *Emotional and Behavioural Difficulties.* 6 (2) pp. 91–101.

Stephen, C. (2010) 'Pedagogy: The Silent Partner in Early Years Learning'. *Early Years.* 30 (3) p. 28.

Stewart, N. (2011) *How Children Learn: The Characteristics of Effective Early Learning.* London: Early Education.

Stringer, E. T. (1996) *Action Research: A Handbook for Practitioners.* London: Sage.

Stringer, P., Stow, L., Hibbert, K., Powell, J., & Louw, E. (1992) 'Establishing Staff Consultation Groups in Schools'. *Educational Psychology in Practice: Theory, Research and Practice in Educational Psychology.* 8 (2) pp. 87–96.

Sylva, K., Melhuish, E., Sammons, P., Siraj-Blatchford, I., & Taggart, B. (2004) *The Effective Provision of Pre-School Education. (EPPE) Project: Final Report: A Longitudinal Study Funded by the DfES 1997–2004.* Institute of Education, University of London/Department or Education and Skills/Sure Start: London.

Vygotsky, L. S. (1978) *Mind and Society: The Development of Higher Mental Processes.* Cambridge, MA: Harvard University Press.

Zuckerman, G. (2007) 'Child-Adult Interaction that Creates a Zone of Proximal Development'. *Journal of Russian and Eastern European Psychology.* 45 (3) pp. 43–69.

11 Developing professional practice through Work Group Supervision

This chapter addresses some important challenges faced by Early Years educators in understanding the observations they make concerning children's development and learning in their play. It also explores how Work Group Supervision allows for reflection and encourages Early Years educators to critically consider the purpose and function of their teaching. Early Years educators are, without a doubt, strongly influenced by their personal and professional knowledge and will have many different ideas about how children learn. Their beliefs about children's learning are central to how they implement and interpret the curriculum framework and they will find many different ways of doing so. For example, they may organise activities where all the children are expected to do the same thing or only observe adult-led activities. How Early Years educators take account of children's needs and interests rather than being ruled by schedules or routine is critical. This will be especially important in how they teach and plan a stimulating learning environment.

Prior to the Work Group Supervision, irrespective of the Early Years educators' ability, they regarded the developmental descriptors in the curriculum framework as the only reference point for what to observe. How they perceived success or failure was determined by this. In this respect, a fear of failure in making observations is the outcome of consciously or unconsciously engaging in making sense of their observations and it is possible to link fear of failure to the influence that policy-makers have on Early Childhood education. Links can be established to the Early Years educators' levels of anxiety over performing in the right way to satisfy curriculum requirements, managers or inspection regulations – this may also influence a fear of failure in observational tasks. How Early Years educators are supported to engage with their fears and develop their knowledge and skills has implications for effective practice.

Observations are important, but so too is the allocation of time and space to reflect on them as a group – this can lead to deep professional learning. Leaders and managers have a pedagogical responsibility to both support and enable professional learning. Work Group Supervision provides opportunities to learn from each other, and supports educators to acknowledge and take responsibility for developing their knowledge about child development. Work Group Supervision is necessary if we are to have a well-trained workforce with the vital knowledge and skills required to help them to deliver the curriculum to children.

Understanding child development is key

Siraj-Blatchford (2010) recognises that Early Years educators encounter many difficulties in understanding children's learning. Not only do many of them lack knowledge of child development and the unique characteristics of children, they also lack knowledge of how to implement the curriculum framework. Manning-Morton (2006) finds that compartmentalising areas of learning is not helpful in supporting Early Years educators to develop a holistic understanding of the children. Other studies show that when Early Years educators only focus on areas of learning they may not see the complexities and connections involved in children's play (Drummond, 2012). As a result, the understanding of children's learning becomes even more challenging. In this extract, Erica reveals the complexity of implementing the curriculum framework as well as insight into what was required of her:

> I'm not interfering in their play as much with most of my key children, I used to think, 'They're not doing very much', or 'I'm worried about why they're not covering this area of learning and doing stuff like that'. Now, I'm just like, 'Well, they don't need to cover it all. You just need to watch what they're doing and their interests'.

This demonstrates that, before the Work Group Supervision, Erica had clearly evaluated her observations based on the curriculum framework outcomes. This resulted in her not thinking about how she was being informed by the children about her next steps and she lacked understanding about how to use the information that she had gathered from observation in her assessment and planning. Rather, her focus was on whether the children had made measurable achievements in relation to the framework's goals, whilst paying no attention to how the information about the child's learning would inform her subsequent pedagogical practice. This also suggests that the group supervision has influenced her responses and subsequent interactions with the children. Most importantly, Erica is demonstrating her beliefs about how infants and young children learn in an environment that supports and values what they can do and are interested in.

Misunderstandings about implementing the curriculum

Interpretation of the responses of the four we have followed in this book, indicates that the focus on regulation and measurement may also have had an influence on how they implemented the Early Years Foundation Stage framework. This created tensions between the process and outcomes of play, development and learning and the Early Years educators' professional and personal values. This is evident in the way they interacted with children and intervened to achieve outcomes within the curriculum framework. Tensions were also created regarding their expectations, understanding and ideas about children's learning.

Moss (2014:43) concludes that "technical practice is dominated by a technical question, 'what works?', with the technique of evidence-based policy and practice supposedly able to supply the right technical answer". He goes on to argue for a different paradigm, one more able to consider ethical and political practice above technical practice. In other words, evidence-based policy can only make sense when it is put into context and interpreted. The quality of Early Childhood provision relies extensively on the political decisions made about early development and learning. Whilst the technical approach has the potential to increase outcomes for children, it is not without risk. In many respects, this emphasis on ticking boxes only works to create children who have been moulded into the shape which adults and cultures desire, through the mechanism of prescribed developmental descriptors. Arguably, the developmental descriptors do not speak for themselves – to be meaningful they must be interpreted in the context of learning and interactions.

In terms of the Early Years educators' professional judgement, the developmental descriptors had been regarded as absolute proof. Because of this, the Early Years educators could avoid having to think about their meaning once they had been seen. This finding is supported by Moss (2014), who suggests that the technical approach does little to encourage an individual's ability to connect personal values and beliefs with practice. This point raises questions about how the developmental descriptors are assessed and the extent to which a technical approach may hamper the ability of Early Years educators to interpret such instructions. Without such considerations of one's interpretations, self-understanding will inevitably be limited, as was the case with the four Early Years educators at the start of this research. This finding reinforces Moss's (2014) call for ethical and political practice. It also links to Frost's (2011) findings that interpretations must be analysed. This may produce multiple perspectives which necessitate making political and moral judgements. Early Childhood education is political and Moss is calling for Early Years educators to have a voice and to be able to question how and why policy-makers make the decisions they do, by providing politicians with evidence-based practice.

Providing pedagogical support

Isolation at work is recognised as a specific issue experienced by Early Years educators, particularly those who lack professional training or feel inadequate (Elfer, Goldschmied & Selleck, 2012). Isolation has been identified as a major contributory factor to lacking confidence in the decision-making process. However, isolation should not be thought of simply as a personal construct in the work circumstances of individual Early Years educators, it is also associated with the culture of the work environment that they enter. This could range from how supportive the leadership team is in Continuing Professional Development opportunities, how breaks and lunchtime are scheduled, whether there is a comfortable staff or work room, if Early Years educators are encouraged to work in pairs, or how effective communication is within the setting.

Here, Erica recalls how, before the Work Group Supervision, she would often withdraw from the process of observations as a way of coping with her insecurities. Following the group supervision, she reflects upon the extent to which her insecurities had affected her competency, challenging herself more consciously to face them.

> It makes me feel good. It makes me feel really good, because you are not just one little pony sitting in a corner trying to do all this work on your own. It makes me feel excited because I'll benefit from a staff meeting now, whereas before I wanted to sit there and just go home. I was like, 'What is the point, talking about some random thing that someone did last week.' So, it makes me feel much better now to sit in the staff meeting and be more positive about it.

Erica's description conveys a sense that she now feels liberated from her self-imposed isolation. The Work Group Supervision gives her a space to focus on her observations and challenges her to stand back, examine in detail what the child is doing, and consider her own response. However, all the Early Years educators participating in the group supervision had also lacked essential knowledge in how to facilitate learning with the children, something that has been found in previous studies with Early Years educators by Pascal and Bertram (1997), Nutbrown (2012) and Wood (2016). Wood and Nutbrown argue that some Early Years educators lack knowledge in implementing the EYFS. Nutbrown also claims that current training does not always equip Early Years educators with the knowledge and skills needed to do their job.

Refreshing and updating knowledge

The Department for Education (DfE, 2014:20) policy statement on the knowledge base of Early Years educators asserts that "the daily experience of children in Early Years settings, and the overall quality of provision, depends on all practitioners having appropriate qualifications, training, skills and knowledge and a clear understanding of their roles and responsibilities". However, the four Early Years educators in this study were found to be unaware of how to identify the significant learning needs and interests of children. They were also unaware of how best to either support or improve the children's learning.

It is important that Early Years educators are supported in developing and expanding their understanding based on their observations of what children are currently interested in. Pascal and Bertram suggest that Early Years educators need to develop and integrate pedagogical approaches which allow them to facilitate children's learning. However, this had been seen as a challenge by the women because they lacked vital knowledge of child development, meaning they were unable to effectively implement the EYFS. We have seen that their knowledge of child development varied, with different levels of understanding on how to implement the EYFS. This gap between knowledge and implementation can be supported by professional dialogue and reflective discussions with colleagues. The Early Years educators in this study indicate that this not only increases their knowledge, skills and confidence, but also gives them a better understanding of themselves and the children.

The tensions linked with making effective observations – as well as interacting with, analysing, interpreting and implementing the curriculum framework – can have an effect on the Early Years educator, sometimes making them feel like a novice, either in their own practice, or when critically reflecting on and talking about it. Proper support has the potential to add to their sense of well-being as they begin to work with others who are also on a similar journey. This has important implications for developing an alternative enabling supervision framework for supporting and sustaining Early Years educators. Knowledge and understanding come through identifying the different aspects of observational work where they need support in order to meet the diverse and individual needs of the children. While the role of the facilitator in guiding the group discussion is not the main focus here, it is important to recognise the key components of this support – being thoughtful, but also welcoming novelty, surprise, and learning within the group. Hopkins (1988), Manning-Morton (2006) and Elfer and Dearnley (2007) recognise the value of group meetings but emphasise the importance of engaging with and containing participants' anxieties.

Conclusion

Work Group Supervision is central to maintaining and sustaining effective observations, teaching and learning. However, it cannot exist in a vacuum, instead it requires a safe and supportive nurturing environment to facilitate adults' learning so that all children benefit from effective teaching. The many decisions that educators make each day about children's development and learning must be informed by knowledge and understanding of how children learn. Work Group Supervision helps educators to improve their practice, develop vital knowledge, work well as part of a team and support each other. It demands that leaders and managers prioritise the dual aspects of supervision, performance and support, which can enable educators to both grow and develop. Providing support to educators through Work Group Supervision is key to supporting their professional development and their emotional well-being.

There is no doubt that the role of Early Years educators can be challenging. However, the Work Group Supervision approach laid out in this book offers leaders and managers a sustainable and affordable way of developing, supporting and improving professional practice. For this reason, the most effective Early Years settings participate in Work Group Supervision. So often they are driven by an ethos and underpinning values that give priority to professional support and learning.

Bibliography

Department for Education (2012) *The Statutory Framework for the Early Years Foundation Stage*. London: DfE.
Department for Education and Health (2011) *Supporting Families in the Foundation Years*. London: DfE.
Department for Education and Skills (2002) *Birth to Three Matters: A Framework for Supporting Early Years Practitioners*. London: DfES Sure Start Unit.
DfE (2014) *The Statutory Framework for the Early Years Foundation Stage*. Runcorn: Department for Education.
Drummond, M. J. (2012) *Assessing Children's Learning*. London: Routledge.
Early Education. (2008) *Practice Guidance for the Early Years Foundation Stage. Setting the Standards for Learning, Development and Care for Children from Birth to Five*. London: Department for Children, Schools and Families.
Early Education. (2012) *Development Matters in the Early Years Foundation Stage*. London: Early Education.
Elfer, P. & Dearnley, K. (2007) 'Nurseries and Emotional Well-being: Evaluating an Emotionally Containing Model of Professional Development'. *Early Years*. 27 (3) pp. 267–278.
Elfer, P., Goldschmied, E., & Selleck, D. (2012) *Key Persons in the Early Years: Building Relationships for Quality Provision in Early Years Settings and Primary Schools*. 2nd. London: David Fulton.
Frost, N. (2011) *Rethinking Children and Families: The Relationship between Childhood, Families and the State*. London: Continuum International.
Hawkins, P. & Shohet, R. (2012) *Supervision in the Helping Professions*. 4th. Maidenhead: McGraw-Hill, Open University Press.

Hopkins, J. (1988) 'Facilitating the Development of Intimacy between Nurses and Infants in Day Nurseries'. *Early Child Development and Care*. 33 (1) pp. 99–111.

Manning-Morton, J. (2006) 'The Personal Is Professional: Professionalism and the Birth to Threes Practitioner'. *Contemporary Issues in Early Childhood*. 7 (1) pp. 42–52.

Moss, P. (2013) *Early Childhood and Compulsory Education: Reconceptualising the Relationship*. London: Routledge.

Moss, P. (2014) *Transformative Change and Real Utopias in Early Childhood Education: A Story of Democracy, Experiment and Potentiality*. London: Routledge.

Nutbrown Review (2012) *Foundations for Quality: The Independent Review of Early Education and Childcare Qualifications. Final Report*. London Department for Education.

Pascal, C. & Bertram, A. D. (1997) *Action Plans: A Guide for Private and Independent Providers of Nursery Education*. London: DfEE.

Pascal, C. & Bertram, T. (2012) 'Praxis, Ethics and Power: Developing Praxeology as a Participatory Paradigm for Early Childhood Research'. *European Early Childhood Education Research Journal*. 20 (4) pp. 477–492.

Siraj-Blatchford, I. (2010) 'Learning in the Home and at School: How Working-Class Children Succeed against the Odds'. *British Educational Research Journal*. 36 (3) pp. 463–482.

Wood, E. (2016) 'Professional Knowledge, Assessment and Accountability: A Perspective from England'. *Early Education Journal*. Spring. 78 pp. 13–15.

Index

accommodation 11
accountability 1, 107, 110
active learning 28–29, 37, 71, 130
Adams, S. 101, 133
adaptation 11
adult-led activities 25, 29, 141, 149
adult role 14, 16
Anning, A. 26
anxiety 63, 75, 80–81, 82, 94, 110, 137, 149, 153
Arnold, Cath 129
assessment 25, 28–29, 36
assimilation 11
assumptions 30, 69, 73, 75, 76, 105
Atherton, F. 47
Athey, Chris 4, 25, 45, 49, 120, 129
Attfield, J. 122
autonomy 139, 140

babies 26, 45–46
Bain, A. 78, 92, 93, 109
Barnett, L. 78, 92, 93, 109
Bayley, R. 135
beliefs 26, 114–115, 122, 128, 149, 150, 151
Bennett, S. 91
Bertram, A. D. 152, 153
Bion, W. 18–19
Bloch, C. 49
block play 41–43, 51
Bowlby, John 4
Bozic, N. 89
brain development 26, 45
Brodie, K. 122
Bronfenbrenner, U. 14, 89–90, 91
Bruce, Tina 30, 49, 120; attitudes to children 26; child development theories 19; Froebelian principles 6, 63; play 27, 36, 39, 140–141; schemas 56, 129

Bruner, J. S. 14
Buldu, M. 135
burnout 72

Callanan, M. 23
Caplan, G. 88, 89, 91
Carter, A. 89
cause and effect 49, 51
Chaiklin, S. 86
child-centred approach 8
child development 2, 19–20, 26, 29–31, 61, 150; Anna Freud 17–18; Isaacs 7; lack of knowledge about 23–24, 28, 153; misconceptions 125; observation of play 30; Piaget 15; training 67–68; Vygotsky 12–13, 14; Work Group Supervision 107, 111–112, 114, 116, 150; writing up observations 127
child-led activities 6, 25, 29–30, 48, 141
Chukovsky, K. 27
Circles of Adults (CoA) 90–91
Clough, P. 79
cognitive development 7, 9, 10–12, 13, 16, 31
collaboration 77, 86, 90, 109; collaborative learning 92, 114, 115, 129; facilitator role 79; group consultation 89, 95–96; Process Consultation 95; Vygotsky 87–88, 92, 95; Work Group Supervision 110, 111, 113
communication 26, 86, 109–110, 115–116; group consultation 95–96; questioning 136–137, 138; self-initiated activities 37; support 152
competence 36, 39
confidence 106, 110, 112, 114, 115–117; children's 140; interaction within the group 108; interactions with children 134, 137, 142; lack of 28, 103, 113, 123, 152; observation 121, 124–125,

156

130; professional dialogue 153; self-understanding 109, 129; well-being 145, 146; writing up observations 126
connecting and disconnecting schema 55–56
construction play 43
containing schema 52
containment 18–19
Continuing Professional Development (CPD) 23, 26, 63–64, 124–125; supportive leadership 152; Vygotskian approach 86; work discussions 92, 94; Work Group Supervision 69, 73; *see also* professional development
counter transference 18
creativity 5, 25, 26, 27
critical incidents 69
critical thinking 29
cultural context 12–13
culture 39, 87, 88, 91
curriculum 2, 26–27, 127, 149, 150, 151

Dalli, C. 26
Davis, G. 93
Dearnley, K. 73, 153; CPD 64, 124–125; emotions 78, 92–93, 135; interaction within the group 108, 109; lack of support 72
decision making 100, 140
deep-level learning 143–144
developmental descriptors 151
Dewey, John 4, 7, 17–18
dialogue 3, 71; Caplan 89; professional 153; Vygotsky 86, 88
discovery 37
diversity 138
documentation 101; *see also* writing up observations
dolls 53
Donaldson, M. 15, 40
drawing 5, 41, 42, 56, 127
dressing up 53
Drummond, M. J. 122

early childhood education and care (ECEC) 26–27
Early Years Foundation Stage (EYFS) 93, 152, 153
educators 1–3, 23–32, 35–36; collaboration 109; interactions with children 132–146; professional practice 149–154; role of 24–26; support for 67–68; Work Group Supervision 1, 61–64, 66, 69–82, 102–117, 120–129
Edwards, A. 26
Effective Provision of Pre-school Education (EPPE) Project 138–139

ego 16–17
Elfer, P. 73, 153; CPD 64, 124–125; emotions 78, 92–93, 135; interaction within the group 108, 109; interactions with children 143; lack of support 72; reactions to observations 32
emotional development 9, 16, 31, 63, 79
emotional health 24–25
emotions 78, 81, 95, 129; emotional demands 135; emotional engagement 72, 82, 107, 132, 142, 143; symbolic representation 48; work discussions 92–93
Empiricism 26, 27, 28
empowerment 72, 79, 80, 82, 105, 106–107, 129
enclosing schema 51–52
enveloping schema 52–54
environment 1, 6, 25
ethical observation 122
evaluation 77
evidence-based practice 151
exploration 37, 47

facilitators 1, 71–72, 75, 78–79, 81, 82, 153; action and decision making 100; collaboration 109; consultation 88, 95; power 80
fantasy 38, 42, 43–44
Farouk, S. 77, 90, 91, 113
fear 63, 75, 80–81, 103
feedback 61, 62, 69, 71; Circles of Adults 90; facilitators 81; stages of Work Group Supervision 76, 77
free play 8, 16
freedom 6
Freud, Anna 17–18
Freud, Sigmund 9, 16–17, 18, 19
Froebel, Friedrich 4–7, 15–16, 17–18, 19, 36, 37, 74, 120
Frost, N. 151

games 36, 39
Gardiner, J. 67–68
Gardner, D. 17
Goouch, K. 23
Grimmer, Tasmin 129
group consultation 85–96
group dynamics 91–92
group size 71
gunplay 63

Hamachek, D. 114
Hanko, G. 77, 86, 89, 90, 91, 109, 113–114
Hawkins, P. 61–62, 69, 77
holding 18, 19
holistic development 7, 29, 73
Hopkins, J. 63, 73, 92, 93, 109, 153

Index

id 16–17
identity 44, 94, 95
imagination 36
imitation 37, 38
independence 25
Inhelder, B. 18, 37, 129
intellectual development 10, 15
Interactionism 26
interactions 1, 132–146
intersubjectivity 87, 93
intervening 31, 135–136, 137, 146
involvement scales 143–145
Isaacs, Susan 4, 7–10, 12, 15–16, 17–18, 19, 120
isolation 109, 152

Jackson, E. 63, 73, 74
joint activity 87, 88, 95

Karmiloff-Smith, A. 15
Klein, Melanie 9, 18
knowledge: child development 30; Early Years educators 25, 117, 121; EPPE Project 138; facilitators 71, 81; group consultation 85; Isaacs 9; lack of 28, 152, 153; Piaget 11, 15; play 37; professional 31, 36; refreshing and updating 152–153; schemas 47, 48; Vygotsky 88; Work Group Supervision 61, 67, 74–75, 77–78, 106, 113, 114, 153–154

Laevers, Ferre 143–145
language: brain development 26; linguistic development 31; Piaget 11–12; self-initiated activities 37; skills 25; Vygotsky 13–14, 87, 91
leaders 36, 67, 68, 69, 152, 154
learning: active 28–29, 37, 71, 130; beliefs about 149; child-led versus adult-led activities 141; collaborative 92, 114, 115, 129; deep-level 143–144; Froebel 4–5, 15; group consultation 85; involvement of children in 141–142; lack of knowledge about 153; observations 122, 123–124; pedagogy 31, 101; Piaget 15, 16; play-based 25, 30, 31; relationship-based 63–64, 77; scaffolding 2; schemas 45; shared 109; visible 124–125; Vygotsky 12, 14, 16, 86, 87–88, 91, 92; Work Group Supervision 68, 71, 75, 81–82, 100, 104–107, 111–112, 116–117, 121, 126–127, 150
Liebschner, J. 36
listening 79, 95–96, 106, 113, 136
literacy 25, 26, 138
Louis, Stella 49, 129

Malaguzzi, Loris 4
malleable materials 43
Malting House School 8–9, 10, 15
managers 36, 67, 68, 69, 76, 93, 154
Manning-Morton, J. 73, 113, 150, 153; CPD 63–64, 77, 124–125; emotions 81, 92; interaction within the group 108; interactions with children 143; Process Consultation 94, 95; theoretical knowledge 74
materials 43, 49, 55, 127, 129
mathematics 37, 42–43, 47, 54, 138
McMillan, Margaret 4
Medwell, J. 26
Melhuish, E. 26–27, 67–68
metacognition 36, 40
modelling 5, 41, 127
Monsen, J. J. 91
Montessori, Maria 4, 17–18
Moss, P. 151
Mother Songs 6
motivation 6, 24–25, 63, 71, 110, 112
motor expression 5
movement 48, 51, 55
Moyles, J. 101, 133
Moylett, H. 29
Murphy, C. 115
Musgrove, A. 101, 133

Nativism 26, 27
needs 25
Newton, C. 90–91, 110
numbers 54
numeracy 25
Nutbrown, Cathy 23, 28, 47, 79, 129, 152
object permanence 52, 53

Observation, Assessment and Planning (OAP) 86–87
observations 2, 19, 23–24, 28–29, 32, 66; connecting with children 137–138; fear of failure 149; Froebel 6; Isaacs 7–8, 9, 16; pedagogy 101; play 27, 29–30, 35–44, 120, 123, 128–129, 135; reflection on 150; role of Early Years educator 25; schemas 45, 46–47, 50–56; starting with 133; support for educators 68; work discussions 93; Work Group Supervision 1, 61–62, 70–78, 81–82, 100–107, 111, 114, 120–129, 153; writing up 125–127
occupations 5
orientation schema 55

Page, J. 93
painting 5, 41, 127, 139–140
Papatheodorou, T. 121
parents 9, 25, 31, 68, 130

Pascal, C. 152, 153
pedagogy 31, 101, 108, 112, 122; EPPE Project 138; interactions with children 140–141, 143; pedagogical support 152
Pestalozzi, Johann 4
phantasy 38
physical development 31, 50
physical skills 25
Piaget, Jean 4, 10–12, 15–16, 17–18, 19, 37, 52, 120, 129
planning 25, 141–142
play 2, 19–20, 25, 31; Anna Freud 17; centrality of 28; free play 8, 16; Froebel 5–6, 16, 36, 37; gunplay 63; interactions with children 133–140, 146; Isaacs 8, 16; Klein 18; meaningful 132; observation of 27, 29–30, 35–44, 120, 123, 128–129, 135; pedagogy 101; Piaget 11; schemas 46–47, 48–49, 50–56, 59; self-understanding 135–136; symbolic 12, 14, 16, 36, 43; unstructured and guided 140–141; Work Group Supervision 104, 107, 117; writing up observations 127
Plowden Report (1967) 18
policy 70–71
positioning schema 54
Powell, S. 23
power 80
pretend play 37, 38, 48–49, 127
problem solving 37, 41; Circles of Adults 90, 91; group consultation 85, 89–91, 95–96; Process Consultation 94, 95; Vygotsky 88; Work Group Supervision 81, 107; Zone of Proximal Development 86
Process Consultation 94–95
professional development: group consultation 85, 91; meaningful 87; support for 68; Work Group Supervision 61–62, 66–67, 69, 103, 117, 123, 154; *see also* Continuing Professional Development
professional practice 149–154
progress monitoring 25
projection 18
psychoanalytic theory 7, 10, 18–19, 92–94
psychodynamic approaches 89, 91
Pyke, Geoffrey 7

quality of care 67–68, 69–70
quantity 52, 54
questioning 136–137, 138
radical enquiry 79

record-keeping 72
Reddy, B. 94
reflection 24, 78; Circles of Adults 90; collaborative dialogue 89; CPD 64; facilitator role 79, 81; group consultation 95–96; Process Consultation 94; relationship-based learning 77; time and space for 150; work discussions 92, 94; Work Group Supervision 61, 62, 67, 71, 73, 76, 100, 113, 116
relationships 1; Bronfenbrenner 89–90; building 133; group consultation 95; psychoanalytic approach 92; relationship-based learning 63–64, 77
repetition 46, 47, 129
resources 49, 55, 129
rotation schema 51
Ryder, G. 93

scaffolding 2, 24, 106
Schein, H. E. 86, 90, 94, 95, 109, 110, 113
schemas 2, 30, 45–59, 123; clusters 56; core and radial 56–58; definition of 46, 56; evaluation 58; identification of 49–50; Piaget 10–11; play 43; self-understanding 128, 129; writing up observations 127
Schon, D. A. 89
science 138
self-awareness 69, 72, 79, 89, 112, 117, 124–125
self-consciousness 110, 133
self-discipline 6, 140
self-esteem 140, 145
self-expression 5, 9
self-initiated activities 37, 49–50, 137
self-understanding 81, 109, 124, 128–129, 151; interaction within the group 108, 113; intervening 135–136; lack of 117; personal and professional growth 82; Work Group Supervision 69, 72
sense making 28–29, 36, 37
sensory development 48
shapes 42
Shohet, R. 61–62, 69, 77
Shore, R. 45, 132
singing 5
Siraj-Blatchford, I. 82, 101, 150
size of group 71
skills 117, 121, 132; EPPE Project 138; pedagogical 101; role of Early Years educator 24, 25; self-initiated activities 37
social constructivism 80, 87–88, 135
social context 12–13, 90, 100
social defence systems 92
social development 7, 9, 14, 15, 16, 31, 63, 138
social participation 5
social skills 25
speech 13, 14; *see also* language
Steiner, Rudolf 4
Stephen, C. 141

159

storying 39, 42
subjectivity 87
super-ego 9, 16–17
supervision 61–64; *see also* Work Group Supervision
support 2, 67–68, 72, 116, 149, 153; for children 134–135, 136–137; Circles of Adults 90; pedagogical 152; work discussions 92–93, 94; Work Group Supervision 62–63, 107, 114, 154
sustained shared thinking 138
symbolic play 12, 14, 16, 36, 43
symbolic representation 40–41, 48, 54, 127, 140
symbols 6, 12, 13–14, 37, 38

technical approach 151
theory 4–20, 128–129
thinking skills 37, 41
thought 13, 14, 49
Tickell Review (2011) 86
toys 5, 18, 141
training 2, 24, 67–68, 82, 152
trajectory schema 50–51
transference 18
transporting schema 54

values 114–115, 128, 129, 150, 151, 154
visible thinking 30, 47

Vygotsky, Lev Semyonovich 4, 12–14, 15–16, 87–88, 95, 120; collaborative learning 92; help from knowledgeable other 77, 93; influence of 19; social activities 114; Zone of Proximal Development 14, 85–86, 89, 90, 91, 94, 135

wallowing 27, 36, 39–40, 44
well-being 24–25; play 30, 44; support 153; well-being scales 143, 145–146; Work Group Supervision 63, 73, 76, 107, 117, 154
Wilson, D. 90–91, 110
Winnicott, D. W. 19
women 28
Wood, E. 122, 152
work discussions 92–94, 135
Work Group Supervision 1–3, 61–64; impact on practice 100–117; implementation of 66–82; interactions with children 134, 136, 137, 142–143; key role of observation 120–129; pedagogical learning 31; principles of 70; professional practice 149–154
writing up observations 125–127

Zone of Proximal Development (ZPD) 14, 16, 85–86, 87, 89–90, 91, 94, 124, 135
Zosh, J. M. 37
Zuckerman, G. 85–86, 124